DETECTIVE DICTIONARY

DETECTIVE DICTIONARY

A Handbook for Aspiring Sleuths

by Erich Ballinger

Lerner Publications Company • Minneapolis

Library of Congress Cataloging-in-Publication Data

Ballinger, Erich.
  [ABC Für Minidetektive. English]
  Detective dictionary: a handbook for aspiring sleuths /
by Erich Ballinger.
    p. cm.
  Includes bibliographical references and index.
  ISBN 0-8225-0721-8
    1. Criminal investigation—Dictionaries—Juvenile literature.
2. Crime—Dictionaries—Juvenile literature. 3. Detectives—
Dictionaries—Juvenile literature. [1. Criminal investigation—
Dictionaries. 2. Crime—Dictionaries. 3. Detectives—
Dictionaries.] I. Title.
HV8073.B34513 1994
363.2'5'03—dc20   93-11882
                                                        CIP
                                                         AC

Manufactured in the United States of America

1 2 3 4 5 6 - I/MA - 99 98 97 96 95 94

INTRODUCTION

"The inspector pulled his hat down over his brow, turned his trench coat collar up, cocked his gun, and crept into the dark cellar, the killer's hideout...."

Readers love the feel of goose bumps and the chills that a good mystery story sends up and down their spines. Horror, sweet horror! Holding their breath, they race through the next lines and pages, eager to find out who did what, and whether all will end well. If you are a mystery lover, then you'll enjoy *Detective Dictionary*—particularly if you want to know more about the ins and outs of a detective's job: the tricks of the gangster trade, for example, and what is meant by evidence, autopsy, and dactyloscopy. Remember that even the greatest detectives use a reference book from time to time. Even they don't know *everything*.

To use *Detective Dictionary*, you should first know that:
- the entries are in alphabetical order;
- words are easier to look up if you check the top corner of the pages (there you'll find the first and last entries of each two-page spread);
- a word in **bold type** means that if you want to know more about this word, look it up—it's another entry;
- at the end of the book is an alphabetical index, which lists many detective-related words found in the book.

If you like, you can read this book just as you would a collection of short stories. Open it to any entry that catches your eye. And don't take all the entries too seriously—many are meant to be jokes. But as a junior detective with a sense of humor, you'll be sure to recognize those meant to be taken dead seriously and those intended to make you die laughing.

ALCATRAZ

In San Francisco Bay, not far from the Golden Gate Bridge, lies a tiny, rocky island called Alcatraz. On this island stands a massive federal prison of the same name. Known as "The Rock," Alcatraz held some of America's most dangerous criminals in the 1930s, 1940s, and 1950s. Escape from Alcatraz was nearly impossible (except, of course, for the heroes of certain films and novels, and for one or two magicians). Alcatraz stopped holding prisoners in 1963. The prison is now one of San Francisco's many tourist attractions.

Alcatraz: Close-up

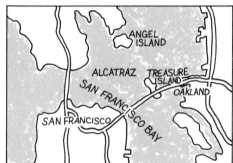

Alcatraz: From the air

ALIBI

If a person can establish that he or she was not at the **scene of the crime**, but rather was somewhere else when the crime was committed, then that person has an alibi.

Alibi interview 1:

Only after checking with Inspector Flatfoot does the detective know that this suspect really was in police custody at the hour in question. His alibi is OK, and he, therefore, could not be the culprit.

Alibi interview 2:

Aha! The top-notch detective notes that most reasonable people don't feed squirrels at 1:00 in the morning, nor can a squirrel vouch for a person's whereabouts. There's something fishy about this alibi!

Here's an assignment for junior detectives: Which of the following alibis stink? (See: Solutions on p. 138.)

ARSENIC

Arsenic is a gray, metallic, extremely poisonous powder. Since it is tasteless, odorless, and almost invisible when dissolved in liquids, it is quite popular with poisoners. And it works quickly. Arsenic is, however, less popular with those who swallow it (see: **poison**).

AUTOPSY

In a white-tiled room, the walls and floor are smeared with sloppily wiped bloodstains. A sweet, rotten smell fills the air. Suddenly, a heavy door slams shut and loud footsteps resound, as they move toward a table in the middle of the room. A scrawny man in a white coat and thick glasses bends over the table. He lifts the sheet, which covers a naked corpse. He stares at the body for a moment. Then he clenches his teeth and picks up a pair of poultry shears. After taking one last deep breath, he cuts open the corpse's chest.

Is this Dr. Frankenstein in search of parts for his new monster? Or a crazy professor? Dracula?

No, it's just another detective: the official medical expert, a type of doctor called a coroner. A coroner's job is to find the cause of a person's death and to discover any unusual circumstances surrounding the death. The unappetizing job of examining the body, which someone must do, is called an autopsy. An autopsy can reveal extremely important information needed by the police.

Here is this coroner's report (without the medical terms):

The corpse: male, approximately 30 years of age; (1)

killed between 3:00 P.M and 5:00 P.M. on Monday, January 22. (2)

Cause of death: a fractured skull from a blow to the back of the head.

Murder weapon: a wooden, blunt object (a club or cleaver handle, for example). (3)

A half hour after the crime, the corpse was dragged into a blackberry bush. (4)

Before being killed, the victim had been made unconscious with a wad of cotton soaked in chloroform. (5)

Shortly before being murdered, the victim took part in a physical struggle, in which he received a blow to the eye; (6)

his opponent received scratches on the face. (7)

We can conclude that the murderer is male, blond, and was drunk at the time of the crime. (8)

Even though the dead cannot speak, it's astonishing how much information a coroner can get from them. How does he or she do this?

Perhaps the medically oriented junior detective can answer some of these questions. Match the numbers given in parentheses in the text with the corresponding coroner's evidence! (1) and (2) have been done for you.

Coroner's Report:

(1) analysis of teeth and bones
(2) stage of rigor mortis (stiffness of the body)
( ) bruise underneath eye
( ) edges of the skull fracture not sharp
( ) bits of cotton with traces of chloroform in
    both nose and mouth, remnants of chloroform
    in lungs
( ) long, thin scratches on the legs, a thorn
    from a blackberry bush in the calf
( ) traces of blood, tiny bits of skin, and
    small hairs under the victim's fingernails
    (traces are not from the victim's own body)
( ) analysis of matter found under the finger-
    nails

(See: Solutions on p. 138.)

NO, NO, NO! I'M NOT AN ENTRY.

I'M DETECTIVE LUCKY,

AT THE MOMENT WITHOUT A JOB—

BUT ALWAYS AT YOUR SERVICE WHEN IT'S A MATTER OF...

CONTINUED ON PAGE 19

B

BEAN SOUP

Cooked soft, this is the favorite dish of hard-boiled detectives. It stimulates both mental and intestinal activities.

BERETTA

This is not a flavor of Italian ice cream, but the name of a weapons company. Beretta has a reputation in detective and criminal circles for its large selection of handguns. Persons who have been threatened or shot with such a device, however, couldn't care less about the brand name.

BLACKMAIL

Two examples of blackmail:

These two examples show how nasty blackmail can be—the victim is totally at the blackmailer's mercy. Blackmail is punishable by law, but since the victim is usually afraid of his own deed being discovered, the blackmailer is usually not reported to the police. The desperate victim often resorts to hiring a private detective. Cases of blackmail must be handled with great discretion.

BLOOD

People who have weak stomachs become nauseated at the sight of blood. Professional detectives, however, roll up their sleeves and get to work the moment they discover a bloodstain. A spot of blood can be a gold mine of information about a person's age, blood type, alcohol or poisons present in the body, and in some cases, even whether the person is a man or woman (see: **autopsy**).

For beginning detectives, it will be enough to determine if that odd-looking, brownish red spot on the tablecloth is plum jam or blood. Here's how:

1. See the entry **laboratory,** and be sure to follow the rules set there.
2. Pour 4 test tubes of water into a container.
3. Add 5 pinches of sodium carbonate and 1 pinch of luminol and stir well.
4. In a second container, pour 3 test tubes of water. Add a few drops of hydrogen peroxide. Stir.
5. Darken room, or wait until nightfall.
6. Pour the two solutions together and dip the piece of cloth with the suspected spot of blood into the liquid.
7. If the spot glows intensely blue, then it's blood!

BOGART, HUMPHREY

Humphrey Bogart (1899–1957) spent half his life in a trench coat with a turned-up collar, a hat pulled down nonchalantly over his brow. He didn't wear this getup during cold, foggy nights on the streets, however, but while roasting under the floodlights of a movie studio.

Humphrey Bogart played the classic film detective in many crime films, such as *The Maltese Falcon* (1941) (see: **Hammett, Dashiell**) and *The Big Sleep* (1946) (see: **Chandler, Raymond**).

Bogart also spent a good deal of time studying the lives of gangsters, since his other famous roles were villains. As a result, he was an expert at dropping dead.

For public relations purposes, Bogart's birthdate was said to be December 25, 1900—although it is unclear why. His fame had indeed little to do with Santa Claus.

BONNIE & CLYDE

In the early 1930s, Clyde Barrow (1909–1934) and his girlfriend, Bonnie Parker (1911–1934), were an unlucky pair of American gangsters. Trigger-happy and brutal, they were never able to pull off a big heist. Stealing cars and holding up stores, gas stations, and small-town banks were all that they ever succeeded in doing. Their largest snatch was no more than $1,500, yet they left a long trail of corpses in their wake. A jaunty Model-T Ford was their favorite means of transportation, filled to the brim with weapons of all kinds.

When they found time, between the rat-a-tat-tat of machine-gun volleys, Bonnie wrote poems and Clyde played the saxophone. They were chased by the law across the length and breadth of the United States. Often wounded, they managed to escape again and again, just in the nick of time. Lucky breaks, nimbleness, and perfect aim were their trump cards. "Wanted: dead-*not*-alive" posters hung in post offices across the country. Organized crime refused to help them—they were merely two "kill-crazy punks."

In 1934, Frank Hammer, an experienced bounty hunter, and a few of his colleagues were able to hunt them down. When the air cleared, Bonnie and Clyde's car had 167 bullet holes in it. For the rest of the day, the public could pay a last visit to the bodies of Bonnie and Clyde. Riddled with bullet holes and smeared with blood, their guns lying across their chests, they offered the world one last thrill.

With a ton of red paint and sentimentality, the story of Bonnie and Clyde was made into a movie in 1967.

BRIBERY

Bribery is the act of offering something, usually money or a favor, to make someone do something that is not allowed or plain dishonest. Bribery is punishable by law for both parties involved—that is, for the person offering the bribe and for the person who takes it. There are two kinds of bribes:

Is the difference clear? What do you think?

C

CAPONE, AL

One of the most famous and disreputable bosses in organized crime, Al Capone (1899–1947) ruled Chicago's underworld in the 1920s. A knife wound on his cheek earned him the nickname "Scarface."

A crime boss is a person of immense power. A small army of specialists in murder, robbery, or drug dealing carry out his commands. A boss has more money than a bank director, more power than a politician, and a whole troop of lawyers to shield him from the long arm of the law.

Everyone knew Capone was a gangster, yet no one could prove it. Capone lived most of his life as a wealthy and free man. When the police were finally able to put him behind bars, it was for not having paid his taxes—a minor offense, considering the number of people he had riddled with machine-gun bullets. But Capone served eight years in prison before he died at the rather young age of 48 (see: **crime doesn't pay**).

CHANDLER, RAYMOND

 Considered one of the best American mystery writers, Raymond Chandler (1888–1959) created the character of Philip Marlowe, a tough Los Angeles private eye (see: **famous detectives**). Among Marlowe's best-known adventures are *The Big Sleep* (1939) and *The Long Goodbye* (1953).

In addition to mysteries, Chandler wrote novels, short stories, and film scripts. Many of his works were made into films (see: **Bogart, Humphrey**).

CHATEAU D'IF

Off the coast of France lies a tiny island on which is located the Chateau D'If. This fortification once housed the grim cells of an intimidating prison from which, it is said, it was impossible to escape. Just the same, in a novel by the French writer Alexandre

Dumas, the Count of Monte Cristo successfully broke out. The story of his flight is breathtaking.

Nowadays, this prison is visited by tourists, sweaty from the heat and from the chills that this gruesome place sends rippling up and down their spines.

CHESTERTON, G. K.

G. K. Chesterton (1874–1936) was an English mystery writer and the creator of amateur detective Father Brown (see: **famous detectives**).

During his boyhood, Gilbert Keith Chesterton was the worst student in his class. For the junior detective who is fed up with school, this may be a consolation. But it should not be seen as worthy of imitation.

CHRISTIE, AGATHA

This Englishwoman was the most successful crime story writer of all time. Agatha Christie (1890–1976) wrote 67 novels and nearly 150 short stories, many of which featured the amateur sleuth Miss Marple or the Belgian detective Hercule Poirot (see: **famous detectives**). She also wrote 16 plays.

A number of Christie's mysteries have been dramatized for movies and television. Especially entertaining are the films starring Margaret Rutherford as Miss Marple, as well as those with Peter Ustinov as Hercule Poirot.

CLOTHING

A detective's clothing has to be inconspicuous. A knee-length trench coat—belted at the waist and with its collar turned up—is recommended. A gray felt hat with a wide brim is worn pulled down far over the brow. (For the traditionally fashion-conscious detective with a European flair, a gray plaid beret can also be worn—again, pulled down over the brow.) A pair of gray sports shoes with thick rubber soles complete the well-groomed professional's wardrobe. In addition, a bulletproof vest, tailor-made (or rather, blacksmith-made), is indispensable. An absolute must, of course, are the 482 sewn-in hidden pockets in which a variety of **gear** can be concealed. Underpants are a question of preference, either in pink or light blue.

Here are a few examples showing private detective C.—and the inconspicuousness of his clothing:

At the beach	At a ball	In the Sahara

...FILLING IN EMPTY SPOTS IN THIS BOOK.   CONTINUED ON PAGE 37

CLUES

Clues are the daily bread of detectives. Everyone, whether they want to or not, leaves some sort of tracks in their wake. Of course, tracks are not always as obvious as those of an elephant that has stomped through fresh snow. Some clues are less visible than the earwax of a baby ladybug.

Important clues are not only obvious ones, such as car tracks on a garden path, **fingerprints** on the murder weapon, traces of blood or other substances on the body of the murder victim (see: **autopsy**), bullets in walls (see: **weapons expert**), and the classic footprint in the flower bed. The detective in search of clues is also interested in hairs on the carpet, cigarette butts, the apple from which a bite has been taken, broken fingernails, the unfinished crossword puzzle in the daily paper, the ashes in the fireplace, and the contents of the wastebasket.

Clues not only have to be found, they must also be secured. They must be analyzed and evaluated by experts, and they may be of value as **evidence** in court. Of what use are traces of lipstick on a wine glass if the expert does not figure out which brand of lipstick it is, where it can be bought, who was wearing it, and what kind of drink was in the glass?

Clues are generally taken from the crime scene by the detective. (Warning: handle with rubber gloves, package separately, label, and date!) If this is impossible, the clues are photographed, sketched, cast in plaster, measured, and described in detailed notes (see: **spelling**).

Here are instructions for the practical junior detective. Footprints can be cast as follows:

1. CAREFULLY REMOVE ALL FOREIGN OBJECTS.

2. ENCIRCLE WITH CARDBOARD SO PLASTER WILL NOT SEEP OUT THE SIDES.

3. POUR IN PLASTER OF PARIS.

4. SET IN WIRE SCREEN FOR STABILITY. COVER WITH MORE PLASTER.

5. WAIT TILL DRY.

6. CAREFULLY REMOVE AND CLEAN PLASTER.

7. LABEL ON THE BACK.

8. RUN! (THAT IS, IF YOU HAVE TRAMPLED YOUR MOTHER'S FLOWER BED!)

COPS & ROBBERS

On playgrounds all around the world, children have played the game Cops and Robbers. Here is one version of this game, which can also be played inside an apartment or house:

You have invited some friends to your birthday party. They have all been given nicknames: Margo "Marple," Ernie the Ear, Sherry "Holmes," and Sally "Spade."

You explain confidentially and secretively (or impishly and with a wink) that someone has stolen your grandfather's hot-water bottle. The crook has yet to be identified. You have, however, received several anonymous notes (who wrote them is not known) that give clues about the thief. Now you ask your guests to help you out with the detective work. Each of them is given an envelope. Margo "Marple" finds in hers:

Margo, who is not timid, goes to the kitchen. Between the pots and pans she finds this message:

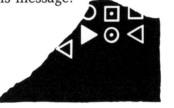

Ernie's envelope contains the following clue:

Ernie runs off and discovers, in an old tire, an additional piece of the puzzle:

Sherry "Holmes" receives the instruction:

And she does indeed find a piece of
paper in the bristles of an old broom:

Skillfully, the parts are pieced together. Baffled and scratching their
heads, the detectives finally figure out that they are undoubtedly
dealing with a **secret code!**

And what about Sally "Spade"?
In her envelope she is told:

Sally hurries off and finds a note in a rusty watering can:

She stumbles down the basement stairs. In an empty wine bottle, another note is hidden:

She has found the key to the secret message! Soon the code has been cracked:

It is quite clear
It was Ernie the Ear

Ernie turns pale. For fun, he is put through an **interrogation** and has to make a confession. He is then given an especially large piece of birthday cake (as a last meal).

You have to prepare this game well:
Write the anonymous notes, hide the clues, think up a secret code, and so on. Most important, don't just copy everything from this book. Change the clues, add details, make the game fit both your surroundings and the number of your guests. Be inventive! But be careful as well—or your house will be turned completely inside out in the search for clues. And don't give anyone dangerous instructions ("The next clue can be found at the top of a telephone pole," for example).
And do without murder cases! For who wants to be a murderer?

COUNTERFEITING

Paper money displays a printed warning that it is illegal to reproduce or copy it in any way. Counterfeiters react to this statement by grinning slyly before getting merrily down to work. The government that prints the bills tries, however, to make the counterfeiter's job as difficult as possible. Most paper money is made with special paper, watermarks, metal fibers, and complicated patterns of multiple colors. Just the same, counterfeiters do succeed from time to time in producing bank notes that are barely distinguishable from the originals. Nevertheless, it is not possible to make absolutely perfect copies. Some tiny difference, often visible only to an expert who uses technical means of detection, always exists.

Counterfeiting rings are difficult to track down, because money often goes through many hands before it is recognized as phony. **Interpol**—an international crime-fighting organization—is often notified, since the rings are sometimes part of an international organization that operates across national borders.

There are many slang terms for counterfeit money: "bogus bucks," "green goods," and just plain "bad money" are a few.

This poor bogus buck will hardly bring its maker luck!

CRIME DOESN'T PAY!

This well-known proverb implies that breaking the law is not worthwhile—that committing crime never brings in a fat wad of cash.

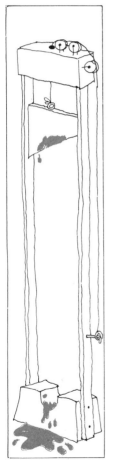

Unfortunately, this doesn't always appear to be the case. Occasionally, a crime boss becomes very wealthy, and he sits by his swimming pool as a highly esteemed citizen in a comfortable villa, snickering up his sleeve. (See: **Capone, Al.**)

But how do we know he is a crime boss? Because—in real life, as in the movies—he always gets caught in the end. (See: **Capone, Al.**)

So the proverb holds true. But we shouldn't need a simple slogan such as "crime doesn't pay" to keep us from a life of crime. Respect for other people, respect for the laws, and respect for ourselves should prevent us from trying to hoodwink others.

CRIMINALS

Just as a person who has no police record has the choice of hundreds of different professions, a criminal has the choice of a variety of careers. To name just a few:

abductor, arsonist, art forger, assassin, bank robber, blackmailer, body snatcher, burglar, car thief, con artist, counterfeiter, embezzler, environmental polluter, fence, forger, gangster, hacker, hijacker, imposter, kidnapper, loan shark, mobster, mugger, murderer, pickpocket, pirate, plagiarist, poacher, purse snatcher, quack, robber, safecracker, shoplifter, shortchanger, slanderer, smuggler, sniper, swindler, tax evader, treasonist, trespasser, vandal....

In the above-listed professions, the possibilities for promotion are very great. The highlight of many of these careers is having one's own office, however small—without a secretary, but with barred windows (often only one).

Here is a task for the junior detective who has a knack for judging a person's character. What are the professions of the persons depicted below, and which of them are criminals? (Note: Appearances are often deceiving!) (See: Solutions on p. 138.)

D

DESCRIPTIONS

A good memory for faces and the ability to describe a person in detail are important qualities for a detective to have—just as important as courage, excellent powers of deduction, and a turned-up collar.

Here is a test for junior detectives who want to know if they have the right stuff:

1. Study the picture carefully for exactly 30 seconds.
2. Cover the picture and answer the test questions on the next page.

3. Compare your answers to the picture. Check the box across from those that are correct.
4. Add up the number of correct answers and put your score in the box at the end of the test.
5. Read the evaluation scale, and let your parents give you a few approving pats on the back.
6. Cheating is definitely not acceptable on a self-assessment test (that is, if you have any dignity at all).

TEST

Put checks in the boxes next to the answers you think are correct. Some questions have more than one right answer.

Shape of face:	
long	
wide	
heart-shaped	

Hair:	
wavy	
straight	
part on the left	
part on the right	
bald	

Eyes:	
close-set	
wide-set	
left eye crossed	
right eye crossed	
not cross-eyed	
eyebrows meet	
eyebrows raised	

Ears:	
small	
pointed	
large	
none	

Nose:	
narrow, long	
bulbous	
cucumber-shaped, shiny	
runny	

Beard:	
full beard, curly	
small mustache, well-groomed	
clean-shaven	
unshaven	
handlebar mustache	

Teeth:	
filling in left bottom wisdom tooth	
right top eyetooth missing	
incisors filed sharp	
should go to the dentist	
left top eyetooth missing	

Special Markings:	
mole on left cheek	
freckle on nose	
dimpled chin	
bullet hole on forehead	

Facial expression:	
lovingly tender	
deviously shy	
brutally cunning	
stupidly grinning	

Name:	
Tristy Chick	
Christy Tick	
Chisty Trick	

Number of correct answers:	

EVALUATION

More than 20 correct answers:

You cheated! There are only 15 correct answers possible!

12 to 15 correct answers:

Did you know that you have a photographic memory? Report immediately to the department of criminal identification! If they don't send you back to your parents, a fantastic career is in store for you!

9 to 11 correct answers:

Wow! You are a young Sherlock Holmes (see: **famous detectives**)! Pass your math classes and nothing can prevent you from becoming a top-notch detective!

6 to 8 correct answers:

Not bad, you just need a little more practice.

3 to 5 correct answers:

Forest ranger and piano tuner are nice professions too—don't you think?

Fewer than 3 correct answers:

It may be time to pay a visit to your eye doctor!

DETECTIVES

Historical Information

As a profession, it's a rather new one—only about 200 years old. In ancient times, not much effort was put into trying to figure out who a wrongdoer might really be. Instead, without further ado, the suspected thief's hand was chopped off, the accused liar's tongue cut out, or the supposed killer beheaded.

During the Middle Ages (about A.D. 476–1450), people asked God to give judgment. For instance, suspects had to run barefoot over a bed of hot coals. If the soles of their feet were scorched, they were guilty. If their feet were not scorched, they were innocent.

Later, things improved—a bit. Suspects were questioned, but in the torture chamber. If they confessed, they died at the stake. If not, they died on the rack.

It wasn't until the 19th century, at the time of François **Vidocq,** that scientific methods were developed to track down criminals (see: **evidence, alibi, fingerprints, autopsy**). Nowadays, the detective accumulates the evidence that can prove the guilt or innocence of a suspect. In the end, though, it is up to a judge and jury to pass the final verdict.

Types of Detectives

The difference between detectives and police officers lies mainly in their **clothing.** The detective usually wears civilian clothes, the police officer a uniform. There are, however, four kinds of plainclothes detectives:

1. Government-employed detectives:

They work for the police (department of criminal investigation, **Scotland Yard,** the **FBI**) in the homicide, drug, or vice squad; they are called all sorts of things: the fuzz, cops, or New York's finest. They patrol streets, help accident victims, and enforce criminal laws. They are sometimes put on serious cases. Most of their time, however, is spent filling out forms, writing reports, and making inquiries. They receive monthly salaries and are entitled to retirement benefits.

2. Private detectives:

They receive their assignments from all types of characters. They conduct investigations on the whereabouts of missing canaries, shadow the wives of jealous husbands, tail the husbands of jealous wives, track down runaway children, and make inquiries about suspicious characters. They are paid daily fees, plus expenses, and a bonus if they are successful. If they stumble

upon a corpse, they have to report it to the police.

3. Amateur detectives:

This kind of detective is found primarily in fiction. They are usually so rich that they don't have to work, and out of pure boredom, or maybe for the fun of it, they spend their time trying to solve particularly tricky murder cases. On their own initiative, they gather information, ponder alternatives in their armchairs, and suddenly know who is the killer. If they report their discovery to the police, they do not usually harvest praise. Instead, the police are often quite wild with rage  (because they didn't figure it out first). If they don't report their findings, amateur detectives make themselves open to even more serious conflict with the law.

4. Junior detectives:

This is what you are, as are most kids your age, at least for a while. But there is nothing anyone can do about it. You are inquisitive, thirsting for knowledge, burning for action, longing for adventure, courageous, and convinced that evil must be revealed and justice done. Later, when junior detectives have grown up,  only a small minority actually become one of the above-mentioned kinds of detectives. Most of them become hairdressers, engineers, teachers, astronauts, beer brewers, politicians, and midwives.

Back to the present: You don't have any clients, but you do have plenty of superiors who get on your nerves. Plus, there are enough unsolved cases, secrets worth investigating, and questionable rascals around to keep you busy.

DILLINGER, JOHN

He robbed banks with the frequency and ease with which most people buy a loaf of bread. Yet John Dillinger (1903–1934) was invariably polite in the process. He would courteously say hello, doff his hat in greeting, and then pin the bank clerk under his machine gun. To female employees, he would express his extreme regret for the disturbance. Perhaps it was due to these manners that he had an unusually good image in the press. Or perhaps it was because in those days, the 1930s, the police were not very popular. The press glorified Dillinger and credited him with robberies and episodes he had nothing to do with. He became a legend. Dillinger fan clubs were founded. When the police finally seized him, Dillinger gave press conferences and held autograph sessions in his cell. His imprisonment did not, by the way, last very long. Armed with a toy gun, he sauntered out of the prison, which was guarded by a whole troop of police officers. His fans cheered, and J. Edgar Hoover, head of the **FBI,** seethed with rage.

A $20,000 price was put on Dillinger's head. The police had the command to ''shoot first, then count to ten'' (even though Dillinger had never killed anyone). He was declared ''Public Enemy Number One.'' Yet the public thought otherwise. Newspapers received many pro-Dillinger letters from their readers.

Despite all the sympathy, FBI agents shot Dillinger four times in the back when he was coming out of a Chicago movie house. Souvenir collectors dipped their handkerchiefs in the puddle of

blood that spread near his body. Crowds of people attended his funeral. And the FBI and the press were at each other's throats for a long time afterward (see: **gangsters**).

Dillinger's story has been told in a number of movies, including the classic 1945 film *Dillinger,* starring Lawrence Tierney.

DISGUISES

Disguises are somewhat out of fashion with modern detectives. Yet the classic detective will, from time to time, try to conceal himself with a tasteful disguise. The basic rule is not to lay it on too thick. Subtle alterations are less conspicuous and can change one's appearance tremendously. For instance:

Detective D., a quick-change genius, demonstrates the art of disguise:

Here is a challenge for ambitious, aspiring detectives: How would you change the appearance of Detective D. so that he is the spitting image of:

 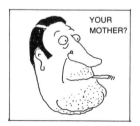 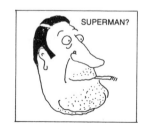

DO-IT-YOURSELF MYSTERY

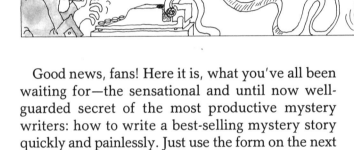

Good news, fans! Here it is, what you've all been waiting for—the sensational and until now well-guarded secret of the most productive mystery writers: how to write a best-selling mystery story quickly and painlessly. Just use the form on the next page, keeping in mind that:

a) The basic text always remains the same.

b) The variables are inserted in the blanks, in numerical order. Select the one you want. In cases of indecision, flip a coin.

c) Even the short sample on the next page gives you 4,782,969 possibilities of putting your readers in suspense. So what are you waiting for?

The basic text:

It was (1) _____

when (2) _____

got out of (3) _____

____. He stuck (4) _____

_____. Suddenly he heard

(5) _____ from

(6) _____ ! As (7)

_____ , he reacted

with the speed of lightning

and ran (8) _____.

Near (9) _____, he

stopped in his tracks. What

he saw made (10) _____

_____. In (11) _____,

(12) _____was lying.

In the next second, he felt

(13) _____. A

hoarse voice whispered:

(14) ''_____ !''

Etc.

① a pitch-black night
foggy and rainy
scorching hot

② Inspector Bumbum
Commissioner X
Detective Rudolf

③ the taxi
the patrol car
the bathtub

④ his pipe in his mouth
his hands in his coat pockets
his finger in his nose

⑤ a piercing cry
the rat-a-tat-tat of machine guns
King Kong roaring

⑥ the harbor
a sewer hole
a transistor radio

⑦ a former rodeo star
a practiced 100-meter sprinter
a karate master

⑧ to the scene of the crime
away
into a dark coal bin

⑨ a dark basement stairway
a vacant lot
the refrigerator

⑩ his blood curdle
him groan
him not give a darn

⑪ a puddle of blood
a garbage can
a whiskey bottle

⑫ a corpse
a Tibetan dagger
his wig

⑬ a gun in his back
hot breath on his neck
queasy

⑭ Stick 'em up
Don't move
Have a nice day

DOYLE, SIR ARTHUR CONAN

Doyle (1859–1930), the creator of the unforgettable master sleuth Sherlock Holmes (see: **famous detectives**), had the misfortune (or fortune) of being less famous than his character. His stories are an absolute must-read for all aspiring detectives.

Doyle was born in Edinburgh, Scotland. He was a physician, novelist, and a killer as well. Yes, he brought Sherlock Holmes to an end by having him plunge down a raging waterfall (in *The Memories of Sherlock Holmes*). His readers were completely appalled, and it is said that some of them even went into mourning for Holmes. Doyle's excuse for killing Holmes—of wanting to direct his literary energies into another channel—was not acceptable to his public. Doyle soon was forced to bring the mystery master back to life (in *The Return of Sherlock Holmes*).

Doyle was honored with knighthood in 1902, for his support of the British during the Boer War (1899–1902).

FUN ASIDE, I WANT TO TELL YOU ABOUT MY LATEST ADVENTURE. IT ALL BEGAN LATE ONE NIGHT...

CONTINUED ON PAGE 47

E

EVIDENCE

Evidence can reveal who a culprit is:

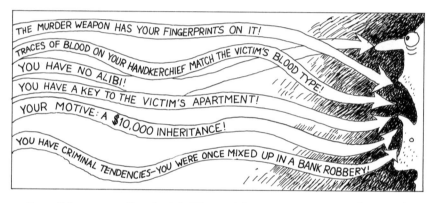

THE MURDER WEAPON HAS YOUR FINGERPRINTS ON IT!

TRACES OF BLOOD ON YOUR HANDKERCHIEF MATCH THE VICTIM'S BLOOD TYPE!

YOU HAVE NO ALIBI!

YOU HAVE A KEY TO THE VICTIM'S APARTMENT!

YOUR MOTIVE: A $10,000 INHERITANCE!

YOU HAVE CRIMINAL TENDENCIES—YOU WERE ONCE MIXED UP IN A BANK ROBBERY!

But did you really do it? The evidence seems to indicate that you did. Yet you haven't made a confession. What verdict will the court come to? Based on the evidence, you may be convicted. Or, for lack of evidence, you could go free.

"Circumstantial evidence" may seem like hard evidence, but it isn't proof. There may be another explanation:

YOU EXAMINED THE WEAPON A WEEK BEFORE THE MURDER.

THE BLOODSTAINS ARE FROM A CHILD WHO HAD A NOSEBLEED.

YOU WERE AT HOME AT THE TIME OF THE CRIME. NOBODY SAW YOU THERE.

THE KEY TO THE APARTMENT? THE VICTIM WAS YOUR CLOSE FRIEND.

YOUR MOTIVE? THERE ARE OTHERS WHO WILL INHERIT AS WELL.

THE ROBBERY WAS YEARS AGO. YOU'VE LIVED RESPECTABLY SINCE THEN.

The experienced detective selects evidence carefully, making sure it is "airtight." He or she then links everything together in a chain of evidence that can be used as conclusive proof.

FAMOUS DETECTIVES

Real detectives of flesh and blood aren't famous. They have no desire to be famous, either, for how would they be able to work undercover? Only detectives out of novels, short stories, and movies are stars. From Los Angeles to Little Rock, and from Stockholm to Sydney, mystery fans know them. The following is a selection of the cream of the crop (in alphabetical order according to first name or title):

AUGUSTE DUPIN

Dupin was one of the first detectives to solve crimes by using pure **logic.** He is known for taking extended walks along dark foggy streets while mulling over a case. When he is finished mulling, he's got the culprit.

Deductive reasoning aside, Dupin's adventures are gruesome, bloodcurdling, and bursting with macabre mysticism. For this reason, these stories can only be recommended to junior detectives who have nerves of steel.

His hobbies: rare books, dark nights
His creator: Edgar Allan Poe, American author
His adventures: *The Murders in the Rue Morgue, The Purloined Letter, The Mystery of Marie Roget*

BALDUIN PFIFF

This pudgy detective loves food and can cuss a blue streak. He has the "pfiff" (German for "knack" or "trick") to follow even the weakest of scents.

His hobby: collecting recipes

His creator: Wolfgang Ecke, German author

His adventures: *A Handful of Thieves, The Bronze Robbers, Visit after Midnight, Enterprise Rattlesnake*

BATMAN

As a comic book detective in Gotham City, a fantasy metropolis, Batman captures villains nightly, hands them over to the police, swings himself into his Batmobile, and then drives off to his subterranean Batcave. Here he discards his batty masquerade to play the part of the well-situated but quite normal citizen Bruce Wayne. His sidekick is Robin, the Boy Wonder.

His creator: Bob Kane, American comic book writer

There are countless other superheroes like Batman on the comic book market: Spiderman, Wonder Woman, Dare Devil....They all fight in fantasy worlds against colorful villains. And the good guys (almost) always win!

DICK TRACY

This tough police detective of the comic strips uses guns, fists, and brains in hunting down crooks. Thanks to a film released a few years ago, Dick Tracy's popularity has soared to new heights.

His hobby: electronic gadgetry

His creator: Chester Gould, American writer

FATHER BROWN

Underneath the black cassock of a small plump priest is a detective of genius. Though he can hardly tell the difference between a footprint and a fingerprint, Father Brown has intuition, an eye for detail, and an understanding of the criminal mind. His only weapon is a large umbrella.
His creator: G. K. **Chesterton**, English writer
His adventures: *The Secret of Father Brown, The Innocence of Father Brown*

HERCULE POIROT

This man with the big mustache is Belgian, and he addresses others as "mon ami" and "mon cher." By his puny appearance and friendly manners, murderers are lulled into a false sense of security, and when they finally realize that they are facing a mental Hercules, it is much too late.
His hobby: reading detective stories
His creator: Agatha **Christie**, English author
His adventures: *Poirot Investigates, Murder on the Orient Express, Hercule Poirot's Christmas, Death in the Clouds*

INSPECTOR MAIGRET

He works hard, to the point of exhaustion, giving all he has for the police headquarters in Paris. Yet he finds the most pleasure in solving cases at home, lying in bed and drinking tea with rum (for his colds).
His hobbies: smoking a pipe and having colds

His creator: Georges **Simenon,** Belgian writer
His adventures: *A Face for a Clue, Maigret and the Headless Corpse,* and more than 80 others!

KALLE BLOMQUIST

Somehow, this young detective manages to be almost constantly mixed up in criminal cases. At those rare moments when he has time, he is a member of the "White Rose" gang.
His hobby: pipes (without tobacco)
His creator: Astrid Lindgren, Swedish children's book author
His adventures: *Master Detective Blomquist; Kalle Blomquist Lives Dangerously; Kalle Blomquist, Eva-Lotte, and Rasmus*

LORD PETER WIMSEY

Wimsey is an aristocratic Englishman who has both the time and money to make the art of detection his pastime. With his irreproachable manners, monocle, and walking cane, he solves the dirtiest of crimes without soiling his white gloves or smudging his black patent leather shoes. Occasionally an offhand judo grip is needed to keep a greasy thug off his immaculate pin-striped suit.
His hobbies: drinking French cognac and choice wines, wearing silk pajamas
His creator: Dorothy **Sayers,** English writer
His adventures: *Clouds of Witness, Gaudy Night, The Five Red Herrings, Strong Poison*

MILO TRBUCHOVITCH

A detective boy wonder who vexes all of gangland with the help of his dog, Stumpi.
His hobby: fishing

His creator: Ellery **Queen,** alias Frederic Dannay and Manfred B. Lee, two American writers

MISS MARPLE

An elderly, good-natured woman, Miss Marple is able to unveil the most lethal of murderers. The criminal world just cannot fathom that a first-rate criminologist is tucked away in this darling lady.

Her hobbies: knitting, eating sweets

Her creator: Agatha **Christie,** English writer

Her adventures: *The Body in the Library, The Moving Finger, A Pocket Full of Rye, 4:50 from Paddington*

Margaret Rutherford as Miss Marple

NERO WOLFE

This giant weighs ⅐ of a ton, speaks 7½ languages, and since 1973 adorns a Nicaraguan postage stamp. It is rumored that he is Sherlock Holmes's illegitimate son. Before he became a private detective in New York, he was a secret agent for the Austro-Hungarian empire.

Nero Wolfe is incredibly lazy and works only so that he can pay his cook and his assistant, Archie Goodwin. The cook satisfies his gigantic appetite, and Goodwin does his detective legwork. Wolfe himself is the brain. He never leaves the house except for professional emergencies.

His hobbies: breeding orchids, breakfast in bed, yellow pajamas

His creator: Rex Stout, American writer

His adventures: *The League of Frightened Men, Black Orchids, Murder by the Book, Too Many Cooks*

PHANTOM

In the African jungle, a Tarzan-like comic book detective adorned with a mask (at such temperatures!) sees it as his duty to put an end to all kinds of criminal monkey business. At his side are a dog, a horse, and an assortment of technical trinkets. He protects the natives and also feels a sense of responsibility for their environment.

Since his birth in 1936, the Phantom hasn't aged a day and still enjoys great popularity. At his zenith, his adventures were translated into 40 different languages, and, statistically speaking, he was devoured by 100 million readers daily.

His hobbies: family life, animals, ventriloquism

His creators: Lee Falk (text) and Ray Moore (artwork), American comic book creators

PHILIP MARLOWE

This private eye knows Los Angeles like the back of his hand. He is constantly at odds with the police, because he is much smarter than they are, and he discovers the culprit before they do. Marlowe is almost always short of money and often has to do without pay, because, in the turbulence of events, his clients are usually

bumped off.

His hobbies: entertaining beautiful women, drinking whiskey

His creator: Raymond **Chandler**, American writer

His adventures: *The Big Sleep, Farewell My Lovely, The High Window, The Lady in the Lake, The Long Goodbye*

SHERLOCK HOLMES

Just the mention of the word "detective" brings to mind Sherlock Holmes. He was born on January 8, 1854, and is still held to be the indisputable champion of crime solvers. After long strolls in London's fog, intensive investigation in his private laboratory, or soulful moments with his violin, he announces who the scoundrel is. His assistant, Dr. Watson, never fails to be flabbergasted. Almost an equal match for Holmes is his antagonist, the ingenious but underhanded Professor Moriarty.

His hobbies: playing the violin, smoking a pipe, peace and quiet (to think things over)

His creator: Sir Arthur Conan **Doyle,** British mystery writer

His adventures: *The Adventures of Sherlock Holmes, The Hound of the Baskervilles, The Valley of Fear, A Study in Scarlet, The Return of Sherlock Holmes*

TINTIN

This pint-sized detective stands his ground no matter how great the danger. Despite human failings, his companion, Snowy, would be an ideal dog for any detective. More often causing problems than not, though, are his two friends Captain Haddock—who is always drunk—and Professor Calculus— who is deaf as a doornail.

His creator: Herge, Belgian comic strip illustrator

His adventures: *The Black Island, Tintin in America, The Red Sea Sharks, The Calculus Affair,* and 19 others

FBI

The FBI (Federal Bureau of Investigation) is the United States' national department of criminal investigation. It deals with incidences of capital crime (murder), counterespionage, and it manages the Department of Criminal Identification. In 1991 the FBI's files contained a collection of 185,458,024 **fingerprints.** (See: **G-men.**)

J. Edgar Hoover, FBI Director, 1924–1972

FINGERPRINTS

The fine ridges on the skin of your fingertips are not the same as those of anyone else in the world, and they will remain the same throughout your life. Because each person's pattern of ridges is

Baby King Kong's fingerprint, left hand, tip of little finger

unique, fingerprints have become an important method of identification.

Whenever someone touches a smooth-surfaced object (the butt of a gun, for example), he or she leaves invisible fingerprints on it. Detectives sprinkle a fine black powder on all objects connected to a crime, then they cover them with a special piece of paper. Any fingerprints left on the objects become visible on the paper. Then the detectives compare the prints to prints of fingerprints in their files for criminal identification. (For each person who has been arrested for a crime, there is a file card with his or her photo and fingerprints.) If an officer is lucky, he or she will find the fingerprint in the file, and the culprit can be identified. If not, the officer tries to get finger-prints from all the suspects. An ink pad and a piece of paper are all that are required. In detective lingo, this procedure is called *dactyloscopy.*

For junior detectives on a limited budget, here is an inexpen-sive way to make fingerprints visible. You just need a bit of soot (blacken an old spoon over the flame of a candle), a soft thick paint brush, and a roll of wide transparent tape.

1. Using the paint brush, gently coat the surface in question with soot until fingerprints become visible.
2. Blow away any extra soot.
3. Cover the surface with transparent tape and press lightly.
4. Pull up the tape and stick it to a piece of white paper.
5. Label the fingerprint with the place and time, and you have officially secured a clue!

Before getting down to work professionally, make a few trial runs following the procedure above.

AS I WAS SAYING, IT ALL BEGAN LATE ONE NIGHT, AS I WALKED THROUGH THE DESER-TED STREET.

HELP!

SUDDENLY...

CONTINUED ON PAGE 59

G

GANGSTERS

"Baby Face" Nelson

Place: *the midwestern United States*
Time: *1930*

A black Ford pulls up to a bank. Three men wearing slouch hats and holding machine guns get out of the car. The driver stays in the car with the motor running. One of the men stands at the entrance of the bank, his gun cocked. The other two enter the bank and explain to the people inside that they are dealing with a small "holdup"—they are in absolutely no danger if everyone behaves.

Somewhere, an alarm goes off. It does not seem to bother the gangsters at all. While one man has the bank personnel covered with his machine gun, the others coolly stuff money into bags. In front of the building, the police and a large crowd have gathered.

The gangsters leave the bank, pushing hostages out in front of them. The crowd cheers, and some even shout "Hurray!" To make the show even more dramatic, one of the gangsters fires a round of shots above the police officers' heads. Rat-a-tat-tat! There are screams and sounds of shattering glass as the crowd takes cover. Shoving money bags and hostages into the car, the robbers take off, tires screeching. Once outside the city limits, the hostages are released and given bus fare for the trip home. Such was a bank robbery in the style of John **Dillinger.**

"Tri-State Terror" Underhill

"Three-Finger" Jack Hamilton

"Pretty Boy" Floyd

"Machine Gun" Kelly

"Boss" McLaughlin

"Killer" Karpis

Edna Murray,
"The Kissing Bandit"

During Dillinger's day, many people lived in extreme poverty. It was the time of the Great Depression, and millions of workers were unemployed, starving, and desperate. "Gangster shows" were the cheapest form of entertainment available. Newspapers and radio stations turned criminals into heroes and each day supplied readers and listeners with new suspenseful episodes.

The poor had no money in the bank, so why should they care if banks were robbed? Bank robbery was a job like any other, only it paid better. The police had few friends during this era, because, in the minds of most people, they protected mainly the rich.

Gangs and gangsters cropped up like mushrooms. Most of them were originally from the countryside, since poverty was particularly widespread there. The most successful gangsters were given nicknames of which they were quite proud—as if these were medals for special achievement.

By the end of the depression, with the FBI's help, these small-time gangsters disappeared almost completely. The only traces left from this period are machine-gun bullet holes on the facades of certain buildings—a favorite sight for tourists. The more famous facades have been carefully preserved and the buildings declared historical monuments.

Yet neither the end of the depression nor the FBI disturbed the larger criminal organizations—such as the **Mafia**—in their enterprises.

To find more information on gangsters, see: Al **Capone, Ma Barker, Bonnie & Clyde, FBI,** and **G-men.**

GEAR

If detectives spend all their time at their desks, they will be low on customers. When detectives are on a case, they have to be out hitting the casinos, bars, nightclubs, boxing rings, train stations, airports, sewer canals, nursery schools, and other seamy locations. And their gear goes along with them, cleverly distributed in their **clothing**—as can be seen in the drawings below of private eye G.

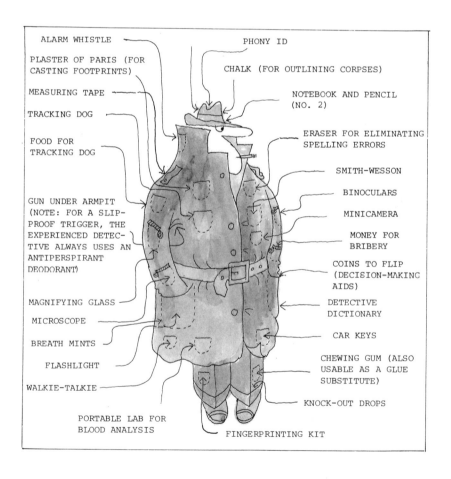

ALARM WHISTLE

PLASTER OF PARIS (FOR CASTING FOOTPRINTS)

MEASURING TAPE

TRACKING DOG

FOOD FOR TRACKING DOG

GUN UNDER ARMPIT (NOTE: FOR A SLIP-PROOF TRIGGER, THE EXPERIENCED DETEC-TIVE ALWAYS USES AN ANTIPERSPIRANT DEODORANT)

MAGNIFYING GLASS

MICROSCOPE

BREATH MINTS

FLASHLIGHT

WALKIE-TALKIE

PORTABLE LAB FOR BLOOD ANALYSIS

PHONY ID

CHALK (FOR OUTLINING CORPSES)

NOTEBOOK AND PENCIL (NO. 2)

ERASER FOR ELIMINATING SPELLING ERRORS

SMITH-WESSON

BINOCULARS

MINICAMERA

MONEY FOR BRIBERY

COINS TO FLIP (DECISION-MAKING AIDS)

DETECTIVE DICTIONARY

CAR KEYS

CHEWING GUM (ALSO USABLE AS A GLUE SUBSTITUTE)

KNOCK-OUT DROPS

FINGERPRINTING KIT

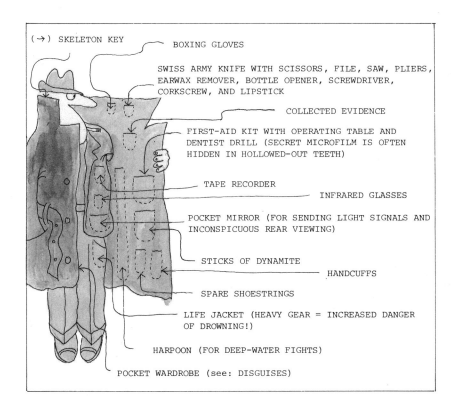

(→) SKELETON KEY

BOXING GLOVES

SWISS ARMY KNIFE WITH SCISSORS, FILE, SAW, PLIERS, EARWAX REMOVER, BOTTLE OPENER, SCREWDRIVER, CORKSCREW, AND LIPSTICK

COLLECTED EVIDENCE

FIRST-AID KIT WITH OPERATING TABLE AND DENTIST DRILL (SECRET MICROFILM IS OFTEN HIDDEN IN HOLLOWED-OUT TEETH)

TAPE RECORDER

INFRARED GLASSES

POCKET MIRROR (FOR SENDING LIGHT SIGNALS AND INCONSPICUOUS REAR VIEWING)

STICKS OF DYNAMITE

HANDCUFFS

SPARE SHOESTRINGS

LIFE JACKET (HEAVY GEAR = INCREASED DANGER OF DROWNING!)

HARPOON (FOR DEEP-WATER FIGHTS)

POCKET WARDROBE (see: DISGUISES)

G-MEN

G(overnment)-men, or G-men, are detectives of the United States government. They are mysterious, feared, and quick with their guns—or, at least, that's their reputation.

The expression "G-men" was first used by the gangster George "Machine Gun" Kelly, when he was encircled by **FBI** officers. He cried: "Don't shoot, G-men!"

Another slang term for FBI officers is "Feds" (for federal agents). Perhaps this term should be given preference—let's not forget all the G-women.

H

HAMMETT, DASHIELL

This famous American mystery writer actually had several careers. Samuel Dashiell Hammett (1894–1961) served in the U.S. Army in World War I and World War II, and he also was a **Pinkerton** detective.

As a writer, Hammett was known for his realistic and fast-moving stories, and for his memorable characters, particularly the private detectives Sam Spade and Nick and Nora Charles. Hammett's most important works are *Red Harvest*, *The Glass Key*, *The Thin Man*, and *The Maltese Falcon*, a classic of detective fiction (see: **Bogart, Humphrey**).

HANDWRITING

BLACKMAIL LETTER

and if you don't pay the $1,000 within 3 days, I'll report you to the police! Bring me the money in unmarked $20 bills.

This letter from an anonymous blackmailer was written quite unevenly. The detective investigating the case obtained samples (letters, notes, etc.) of the handwriting of the suspects, and took them, together with the blackmail letter, to a handwriting expert (graphologist).

SAMPLE I	SAMPLE II	SAMPLE III

The graphologist's analysis proved that the blackmailer had tried to disguise his or her handwriting. While the blackmail letter had been written with the left hand, the person who wrote it was right-handed. According to the graphologist, the writer of Sample II is the person who wrote the letter. The person is probably male, with a withdrawn personality, lacks willpower, and is inclined to swindle.

And how does the graphologist know all this?

The graphologist examines the size and shape of the letters, the amount of pressure put on the pen, the shape of the letters, the distance between words and letters, the relationship between the heights of the different letters, the distance between the lines and how straight they are, the size of the margins, and many other features.

Your handwriting changes slightly with your moods, such as when you are angry, pleased, or afraid. In a similar manner, handwriting may reveal a person's temperament and character. But certain features of a person's handwriting remain constant, even when someone tries to disguise his or her writing.

If the blackmailer had typed the letter on a typewriter, he or she would not have been much more successful. A typewriter specialist can determine the brand, model, and year of the typewriter used, just by looking at the typed words.

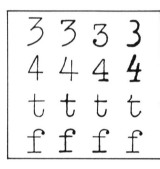

DIFFERENCES IN NUMBERS
AND LETTERS
OF VARIOUS MODELS
OF TYPEWRITERS

The letters typed on different typewriters of the very same brand, model, and year can reveal tiny inconsistencies.

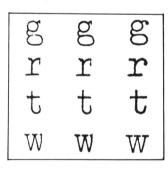

DIFFERENCES IN LETTERS
TYPED ON SEVERAL
TYPEWRITERS OF THE
SAME BRAND

And if the blackmailer claims that the letter was not typed by him or her, but by someone else, the expert can disprove the criminal by examining recurring errors and other idiosyncracies in typing style.

With a magnifying glass and a keen eye, the graphologist can also detect false signatures. Forged signatures are often shaky, lack boldness, and are irregular in thickness of stroke. Both the beginning and the end of a stroke often reveal significant deviations:

Junior detectives who know a thing or two about handwriting can surely detect which of the following signatures have been forged:

(See: Solutions on p. 138.)

HIMES, CHESTER

Chester Himes (1909–1984) was an African American who wrote mysteries that take place in Harlem, a neighborhood in New York City. Himes once served 20 years in jail for robbery, and in his books heroes are scarce. Two detectives, Grave Digger Jones and Coffin Ed Johnson, play merely minor roles. Invariably more important is some poor fellow who has been singled out more or less by chance. One of Himes's characters, for example, is Jackson: a fat, short-legged, and somewhat empty-headed man, who sweats profusely and wets his pants when he is frightened. He is neither a good guy nor a bad guy, but is constantly on the run to save his life. We run along with him, through his dog-eat-dog world.

Some of Himes's works are *Cotton Comes to Harlem, The Crazy Kill, The Heat's On, The Real Cool Killers,* and *A Rape in Harlem.*

HITCHCOCK, ALFRED

 Alfred Hitchcock (1899–1980) is the unsurpassed grand master of mystery films and thrillers. He was born in England and made his first movies there. Then he came to the United States, where he made dozens more movies, and eventually became a U.S. citizen. In the 1950s and 1960s, Hitchcock directed and hosted two series of suspense programs for television.

Alfred Hitchcock's stories are for movie fans who don't mind sitting on the edge of their seat, ready for the next scare. Some of his most frightening films are *Spellbound, Strangers on a Train, Rear Window, Vertigo, Psycho, The Birds,* and *Torn Curtain.*

CAUTION: The name Hitchcock is often used for advertising purposes. A number of mystery novels carry his name, although he himself was not their author.

HOMICIDE

The killing of a person is called homicide. But homicide isn't always murder. It is important to distinguish between the different types of killing—murder, manslaughter, and other classifications of homicide:

1. *1st-degree murder* is the deliberate causing of the death of another that involves malice (wickedness, cruelty, and a disregard for the

consequences of one's actions) and premeditation (planning of the crime). Also, a killing that occurs during the commission of a dangerous felony is considered 1st-degree murder. (A dangerous felony is a serious crime that may cause a person bodily harm, such as arson, burglary, or robbery.)

2. *2nd-degree murder* involves malice, but the murder was unpremeditated.

3. *Voluntary manslaughter* does not involve malice, although the killing was intentional. For example, a situation in which two people are quarreling and one person kills the other in a fit of rage would be considered voluntary manslaughter.

4. *Involuntary manslaughter* is a killing that is committed accidentally, through an act that is unlawful but not a dangerous felony. Involuntary manslaughter can also happen when a person is killed as the result of a lawful act done in an unlawful or reckless manner.

5. *Justifiable homicide* occurs when a person is physically assaulted and defends himself or herself, killing the attacker. Other kinds of justifiable homicide are killing to protect close family members from serious injury or death, and killing a person to prevent a felony.

6. *Excusable homicide* is a killing that occurs completely by accident.

I

IDENTIKIT PICTURE

"Yes, of course! I know exactly what the fellow looked like," asserts the elderly man whose wallet has been stolen. Okay then, describe him. "Well, ah...I mean...how should I put it...sort of like...." And that's about it. If only the crook had had a particularly distinguishing feature—a long nose, a mole, or a dimple in his chin. But no, he had nothing of the sort. How inconsiderate of him!

The police officer gets the huge notebook containing drawings of all the different parts of the face in all shapes and sizes. He and the robbery victim begin the tedious task of putting together an identikit picture. Just as with some picture books for toddlers, the pages are divided into sections that can be flipped independently from one another. The officer and the man try out different combinations until the face produced resembles the thief's.

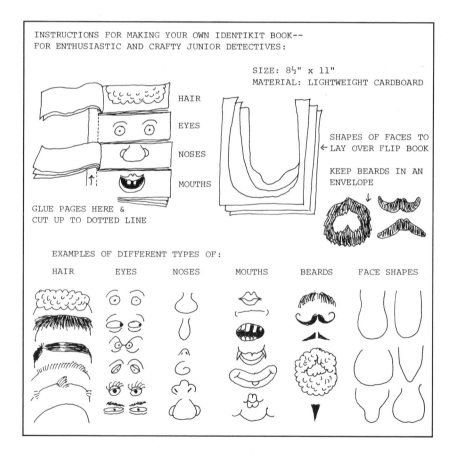

INSTRUCTIONS FOR MAKING YOUR OWN IDENTIKIT BOOK--
FOR ENTHUSIASTIC AND CRAFTY JUNIOR DETECTIVES:

SIZE: 8½" x 11"
MATERIAL: LIGHTWEIGHT CARDBOARD

HAIR

EYES

NOSES

MOUTHS

SHAPES OF FACES TO
← LAY OVER FLIP BOOK

KEEP BEARDS IN AN
ENVELOPE

GLUE PAGES HERE &
CUT UP TO DOTTED LINE

EXAMPLES OF DIFFERENT TYPES OF:

HAIR   EYES   NOSES   MOUTHS   BEARDS   FACE SHAPES

...SUDDENLY,   I HEARD A SCREAM.   FEARLESSLY, I EN-TERED THE BUILDING...   AND FOUND MYSELF IN THE DARK!

CONTINUED ON PAGE 64

INTERPOL

This abbreviation stands for INTERnational POLice. The organization was founded in 1923 and has its headquarters in Paris.

Freddy the Freak has done it again. He has looted a bank in Chicago, and with a booty of $3 million, he is now sitting comfortably on a plane on his way to Mexico City. He had no problems getting through the American passport control at the airport, and in Mexico—well, it's another country with a different police force. The bank robbery in the United States is none of their business, and anyway, they don't know anything about it. At least, this is what Freddy thinks. But he's wrong. Police headquarters in Chicago has already informed Interpol offices all over the world. They have Freddy's name, photo, fingerprints, and they know how much money he stole.

Unsuspecting and whistling cheerfully, Freddy gets off the plane in Mexico City. Suddenly, he feels the heavy hand of the Mexican detective Nico Knattertono on his shoulder, and a gun barrel presses into his back.

Interpol deals primarily with crimes concerning drugs, **counterfeiting,** and internationally organized crime (see: **Mafia**). A small-fry like Freddy is disposed of with a mere flick of the wrist.

About 160 nations of the world are members of Interpol, but many more are not, which is one reason that crooks are successful in slipping through the fingers of the police (see: **crime doesn't pay**) every now and then.

INTERROGATIC

Interrogation is not usually as awful as pictured above, except in movies. In the typical movie interrogation, the suspect's tongue is parched, sticking to the roof of his or her mouth. Sweat pours down the suspect's face, as he or she is bombarded with questions nonstop. That's Hollywood—the dream (or nightmare) factory.

Of course it's true that in a real interrogation, a suspect is not treated to an armchair, coffee, and an air conditioner. But the law does set limits for the interrogating officer. He or she is forbidden to mistreat the suspect, to use a **lie detector** or hypnosis, to administer drugs, to deceive, or to make threats or promises. A confession that has been forced by one of these methods can be challenged in court.

But an interrogation is not merely a pleasant chat—not by a long shot. The interrogating officers have to be on their toes. They have to take the personality of the suspect into account, to appear sometimes tough and sometimes considerate, to observe physical reactions, to be suggestive, to lay traps, to dissect, confuse, probe, encourage, play dumb, play smart, console, insist, seem uninterested, and at the same time lie in wait like a tiger. Most important, they have to be good listeners. It's not surprising that during long sessions of interrogation, the interrogating officers are relieved by their colleagues. (When *their* tongues are parched and stick to the roofs of *their* mouths and sweat pours down *their* faces....)

INTERROGATION

Here is a task to test the interrogating abilities of ingenious junior detectives. Just read the following article and report.

Bank Robbery in Brooklyn!

AP/NEW YORK. Yesterday, Nov. 28, at 9:35 A.M., Security Savings & Loan on 24th Street in Brooklyn was held up by five masked persons, all of them armed. The gangsters were able to flee with the small sum of $250. A bank clerk suffered a slight bullet wound. The police suspect that the gangsters were

TOP SECRET! CONFIDENTIAL!

Interrogation Report
Nov. 30th

Interrogating Officer: Inspector Victor Sneek
Suspect questioned: Thomas ("Tom") Indelicato

Inspector: O.K., Tom, take a seat. It won't take long--just a few routine questions.

Tom: Fire away, Inspector! But not with your revolver! Ha, ha! --Sorry, sir, just a little joke. So tell me, where does the shoe pinch?

I: I'm the one asking the questions here. Where were you on Nov. 28th between 8:00 and 10:00 in the morning?

T: The 28th? Let me see.... Ah, yes! I slept until 8:30. You know, Inspector, I'm not an early bird--not at all astonishing with my profession--~~barem~~ bartender. I close the place down at around 1:00 in the morning. And then the books have to be done, and, well....

I: Keep to the point, Tom!

T: Sorry, sir! So--8:30. Then I ran down to Henry's Diner for a good breakfast. A good breakfast, I always say--

I: Someone in the joint who can confirm your alibi?

T: Sure. Henry himself, the owner. And Charlotte, the waitress. We always flirt around a bit, I'll tell you--

I: Tom!

T: Sorry, sorry. Aw, come on, Inspector, what's this all about? I have a right to know why I'm being questioned.

I: A bank robbery. 24th Street, Brooklyn.

T: (whistles through his teeth) Let me tell you right off the bat, I had nothing to do with it! I didn't even know it happened.

I: Is that right, Tom? It was written up big in all the papers.

T: I don't read the papers. Tell me, did they make off with a lot?

I: Like I said, I'll ask the questions around here. But how did you know that more than one person was involved?

T: Um, why do you ask that? I have no idea....

I: But you asked, "...did <u>they</u> make off with a lot?"

T: Oh, uh, I mean, bank robberies are usually ~~teem~~ teamwork....

I: Okay, okay. Tell me more about your alibi.

T: Oh, yeah. Where was I? Ah, yes--breakfast until 9:00, then off to work. I open the bar at 10:00. Satisfied?

I: Maybe. But it doesn't take you more than a half hour to get to work, does it?

T: Inspector, I.... I would never do anything like that!

I: What about the Savings & Loan Bank five years ago?

T: I did my time for that! I've been on the level since, and I wouldn't dirty my fingers for a few hundred lousy dollars!

I: Now cool down. I only want to know how long it takes you to get to work.

T: Normally a half hour, unless traffic is heavy. And it takes me another fifteen minutes to get the bar ready to open. So you see, I couldn't have been at the bank at 9:35.

I: That will do, Tom. That's enough.

While Tom signs the report, Inspector Sneek snickers constantly. He is sure that Tom took part in the holdup.

How has Tom given himself away? (See: Solutions on p. 138.)

AS MY EYES ADJUSTED TO THE DARK,

I BEGAN TO SEE THE VERY STRANGE OBJECTS AROUND ME.

CONTINUED ON PAGE 67

JUST EMPTY SPACE OR INVISIBLE WRITING? THAT'S THE QUESTION!

INVISIBLE INK

Amateur detective Pauly V., nicknamed "The Nose," was hot on the trail. He nimbly slid down a roof, slipped into a sewer hole, crept along on his stomach through a drainpipe, and reached the hideout of the counterfeiting ring through the ventilation shaft. Drat! The birds had flown! But hidden between bundles of phony bills (see: **counterfeiting**), he found a small book. The word "addresses" was written on its cover. Pauly stuck the book into one of his 56 coat pockets. He heard approaching footsteps and made off.

It wasn't until he was home in his workroom that Pauly found time to look closer at the small book. He opened it and flipped through its pages—and then froze. Mouth agape, eyes bulging, he stared. What did he see? The name and address of the boss of the counterfeiting ring? No. He saw nothing, absolutely nothing. The pages were completely empty!

Here, the experienced junior detective smiles knowingly, nods, and murmurs, "Invisible ink."

Pauly soon understood as well. He slowly came back to life, his eyes receded back into their sockets, his mouth snapped shut. "The Nose" rushed into his **laboratory.** He held the pages of the book over the flame of a Bunsen burner. Soon a clumsy but readable print became visible, and with it, the addresses of many wanted criminals.

Here are two invisible ink recipes for junior detectives who delight in experiments. Be sure to read the **laboratory** entry before you begin!

1. Dissolve a few crystals of copper sulfate (see: **laboratory**) in a few drops of water.
2. Dilute the solution with water, adding a few drops at a time until it is very pale blue.
3. Write with a paint brush on blue paper. Let it dry.
4. To make the writing visible again, hold the paper over an open bottle of liquid ammonia (see: **laboratory**). The ammonia vapors will react with the copper sulfate solution, making the writing appear dark blue.

Use ammonia only in a well-ventilated area! Ammonia fumes can be dangerous!

1. Fill a test tube with 1 cm of water.
2. Dissolve a few cobalt-chloride crystals in it.*
3. Using this solution and a paint brush, write a message on pink or white paper.
4. Wait for the solution to dry, and watch your message disappear!
5. To make the message visible, hold the paper over a small flame (*not too closely,* or it will burn). On pink paper, the writing will appear blue; on white paper it will appear black.

  * You can get the same results by mixing onion and lemon juice instead of the cobalt-chloride crystals and water. (Onion juice is available at most grocery stores.)

J

JACK THE RIPPER

In 1888 a deranged murderer prowled the streets of London. He was called "Jack the Ripper" by panic-stricken Londoners because he slashed his victims' bodies with a knife. **Scotland Yard** arrested three suspects, but the police never could prove any of them had committed the five murders. Jack the Ripper was never captured.

Marie Belloc Lowndes wrote a book based on the case of Jack the Ripper, called *The Lodger,* which Alfred **Hitchcock** later turned into a movie.

ODD!

BIZARRE!

EXTRAORDINARY!

CONTINUED ON PAGE 78

JAMES BOND

This suave character has been around since 1953, when he made his first appearance in a novel by Ian Fleming. But it wasn't until the films starring Sean Connery (and other films, later) that he became famous: James Bond, British secret agent 007. Impeccably dressed, freshly washed and shaven, hair neatly combed and sprinkled with cologne, Bond combats the dirty tricks of enemy **agents** and infernal villains of high caliber. With razor-sharp **logic** and split-second timing, 007 always wins in the end. The action-packed films—including *Dr. No*; *From Russia, with Love*; *Goldfinger*; *Thunderball*; *You Only Live Twice*; and *Octopussy*—delight in presenting all sorts of modern technological gadgets.

If the junior detective who enjoys movies would like to analyze a James Bond film (for purely professional reasons, of course) and his superiors object, perhaps the following fact will be of help: John F. Kennedy was an enthusiastic Bond fan and still became president of the United States.

Author
(Ian Fleming)

James Bond
(Sean Connery)

James Bond
(Roger Moore)

James Bond
(George Lazenby)

James Bond
(Timothy Dalton)

(James Bonds of the future?)

K

KIDNAPPING

On March 1, 1932, at 8:00 in the evening, Charles and Anne Lindbergh put their 1½-year-old son, Charles, to bed. The Lindberghs were a wealthy, respected, and famous couple. In 1927, father Charles Lindbergh was the first person to make a solo flight across the Atlantic Ocean, from New York to Paris. They lived on an estate in the New Jersey countryside.

At 10:00 the family governess discovered that the baby was missing. On the windowsill of the child's room lay a bit of dirt from the garden and a letter stating that the child had been taken. He would be returned to his parents unharmed, the letter said, upon their payment of a ransom. The kidnappers would contact the parents later to set the sum and the terms of delivery. A ladder—which the kidnappers had made for themselves, and which was exactly the length needed to climb into the child's room—was found behind the house. The kidnappers had worn gloves, so there were no fingerprints.

The next day, an army of police officers, detectives, and secret agents swarmed the house and began to investigate the case. Probably scared off by the throngs of people, the kidnappers did not contact the parents. Days went by. Newspapers covered the case daily with front-page updates.

Finally the kidnappers gave instructions. Though the parents left the requested amount of money at the appointed location, the child was not returned.

Mr. and Mrs. Lindbergh

Weeks went by. The Lindberghs paid an additional ransom, but their child was still not returned to them.

It was as if every detective in the country was on the case, trying to track down the criminals. Even the big bosses of organized crime had offered to use their connections in the underworld to help find the child and his kidnappers.

On May 12, eight weeks after the kidnapping, little Charles Lindbergh was found dead in a nearby woods—killed by a blow to the head. He had been dead since a few days after he was kidnapped.

About two years later, police arrested Bruno Hauptmann for the kidnapping and murder of the Lindbergh baby. Hauptmann was convicted and executed for the crime.

Charles Lindbergh, Jr.

This is a famous and unfortunately true case of kidnapping. Kidnapping victims are often called ''hostages,'' and, when a vehicle is involved, the crime is sometimes called a ''hijacking.'' The term ''skyjacking'' is used if the vehicle is an airplane (see: **terrorism**).

KNOW-HOW

As a detective, you must have a few good tricks up your sleeve. Tricks can't replace experience and thoroughness, but they can make the harsh life of the harassed private eye easier. A quick reach into your box of tricks could someday save you from a punch in the nose.

The know-how illustrated here should inspire you to come up with ideas for your own tricks. Tricks of your own design have a great advantage: no one else knows them.

Watch your shadow—it can be a despicable traitor (see: **tailing**).

Old staircases usually won't creak if you edge up them along the wall.

Here is a way for you to determine whether a door was opened in your absence. (Overzealous cleaning personnel can easily ruin this trick!)

Don't rely on footprints! Even they can lie! (See: **clues**.)

Everyday objects can be used as secret hiding places.

A bad cold or a handkerchief over the telephone mouthpiece can make it difficult to identify the voice of the speaker.

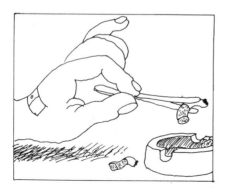

Use a tweezers to touch objects that may be clues.

Well-camouflaged microphones may pick up surprising conversations. (But note: secret recordings may not be allowed as evidence in court. You must have permission issued by a judge.)

Inconspicuously dropped peanut shells are sure to give away someone who is nearing you. (This trick is not recommended for indoor use.)

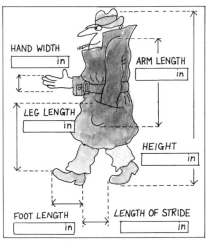

A measuring tape kept in your pocket is indispensable, yet it is good to know your own measurements by heart. You will then be able to measure things with your body without anyone noticing.

Hold a mirror in a book and pretend to be reading. You can now watch a suspect with your back turned. (Title of the book used here: *A Knife in the Back*.) (See: **tailing**.)

To hide from the person you are **tailing,** pretend to search for something in your inner coat pocket!

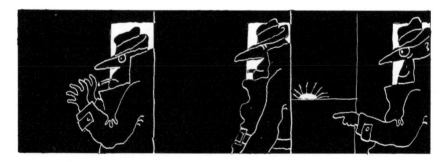

When you enter the dark after having been in the light, close your eyes for 10 seconds. When you open them again, your eyes will adjust more quickly. Detective K. once held his eyes shut for 32 minutes. His vision was great afterward. So was the head start of the person he was pursuing!

A garden hose can uncover buried treasure. Patches of lawn that have recently been dug up are a different color than the surrounding lawn, and water soaks in more quickly!

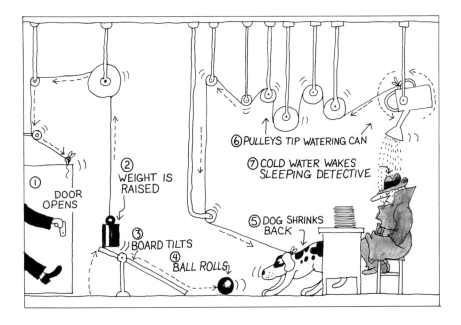

Here is a simple alarm system for detectives in need of sleep. (It alerts one to the approach of revenge-seeking ex-convicts, thieves who want to swipe evidence, and snooping superiors.)

Try observing someone through holes cut in a newspaper. (This trick is so old, that...)

L

LABORATORY

If you are a practical-minded junior detective with a well-developed sense of order, you already keep your living quarters in a more or less tidy state. You may also want to set up one corner in which your detective gear is neatly arranged and handy at all times. Space for a laboratory is also essential. Be sure that your laboratory area has good ventilation. And although an electric barbed-wire fence is not necessary, protect your pets and smaller sisters and brothers by keeping chemicals well out of reach. Label chemicals clearly, and label poisonous chemicals with a skull and crossbones, and flammable chemicals with a flame.

On the next page is a possible arrangement—the office and laboratory of young Detective L.

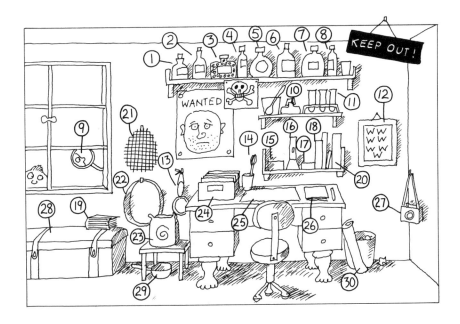

1 luminol (see: **blood**)
2 sodium carbonate (see: **blood**)
3 hydrogen peroxide (see: **blood**)
4 cobalt-chloride crystals (see: **invisible ink**)
5 copper sulfate (see: **invisible ink**)
6 liquid ammonia (see: **invisible ink**)
7 alcohol—always close tightly and keep at least ten feet from any open flame or stove!
8 soot (see: **fingerprints**)
9 a mirror mounted outside the window (it can warn you when friends, enemies, or piano teachers are approaching)
10 Bunsen burner (see: **invisible ink**)
11 test tubes
12 framed copy of the **seven golden questions** (with a secret hidden compartment in the frame)
13 magnifying glass
14 thick paint brush (see: **fingerprints**)
15 ink pad (see: **fingerprints**)
16 flashlight
17 measuring tape (see: **clues**)
18 dictionary (see: **spelling**)
19 identikit (see: **identikit picture**)
20 *Detective Dictionary*

21 metal screen (see: **clues**)
22 cardboard ring (see: **clues**)
23 plaster of paris (see: **clues**)
24 fingerprint file (see: **fingerprints**)
25 plastic sheet (to protect your desk against chemical stains)
26 notebook
27 camera (see: **clues**)
28 box for **disguises**
29 bowl for mixing plaster of paris (see: **clues**)
30 wide transparent tape (see: **fingerprints**)

IMPORTANT TIPS
FOR CHEMO-DETECTIVES

- All chemicals listed here are available at a pharmacy or drugstore.

- Wash your hands well after each experiment!

- Attempt only the experiments explained in this book! Further experiments should only be done in the presence of an adult who has had experience with chemicals!

- Label all bottles and tubes. Keep them closed and out of reach of small children!

- Don't eat or drink while working in your chemistry lab!

THEN, SUDDEN-LY, I HEARD:

DIE, DISGRACED ONE!

I DECIDED TO TAKE ACTION...

CONTINUED ON P. 84

LEBLANC, MAURICE

Maurice Leblanc (1864–1941) was a French mystery writer who did not have a detective as the hero of his stories (as would be usual), but a con artist: Arsène Lupin, a fantastic thief, who robs only the rich and is charming to women and children. Lupin's greatest pleasure is giving the police the runaround, which makes them boiling mad and makes their faces turn the French national colors: blue, white, and red.

Leblanc wrote about 30 books. Many of his stories are collected in the volume *The Extraordinary Adventures of Arsène Lupin, Gentleman Burglar.*

LIE DETECTOR

We say to young children, "You're lying, I can tell by the expression on your face." In using lie detectors, we presume that even adult rascals can't lie without being at least a little bit nervous. Nervousness can't always be seen in someone's facial expression, however, but it can be observed in other ways: by a rapid pulse rate, irregular breathing, and perspiration. The lie detector relies on these symptoms. It is a device that measures a person's pulse rate, respiration rate, blood pressure, and perspiration, when he or she is asked a series of questions. The lie detector records these physical responses on a strip of paper. The interrogating officer can then determine which questions caused the tested person to react with physical signs of nervousness. The results tell the officer whether the suspect was lying.

The junior detective in search of truth may recognize the shortcomings of this method—a person doesn't have to be lying to be nervous. Any quiz or test can do the trick as well. Since the conclusions drawn can be misleading, many places prohibit using lie detectors in the **interrogation** of a suspect, and the results of a test are often not allowed as evidence in court.

When sizing up a suspect, it may be best to rely on keen observation, detailed investigation, and your own judgment of human character.

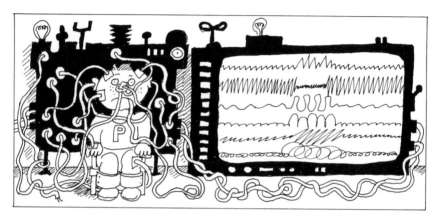

Peter P. is hooked up to a lie detector and asked: "Peter Piper, did you pick a peck of pickled peppers?" Is he lying?

LOGIC

Criminal Inspector Zack has just made a good catch. These four ex-cons from the Viennese underworld are old acquaintances of his—he has helped send them to the cooler several times. This time Zack wants to check their **alibis**. A candy store was broken into last night at 8:00, at the Naschmarkt (an open-air market in Vienna). No money was stolen, but tons of chocolate kisses, sugarcoated almonds, marzipan "Mozart balls," peppermint sticks, and bubble gum disappeared. And Zack is sure of one thing: one of these fellows in custody was at the Naschmarkt last night. But the question is, which one of them?

Zack asks each one where he was at 8:00 the previous evening. These devious characters don't lie outright, but they do try to throw Inspector Zack a bit of a curve.

ALBERT THE APE

I'M NOT QUITE SURE.... I WAS EITHER AT THE MOVIES OR AT A FOOTBALL GAME.

CANDY CHARLIE

I CAN'T REMEMBER A THING!

BURGLAR BURT

I WAS AT A FOOT-BALL GAME. I SWEAR!

DANDY DANNY

I ONLY KNOW THAT I WASN'T AT HARRY'S HAMBURGER STAND AND THAT EACH OF US WAS ALONE AT ONE OF THE PLACES MENTIONED.

No more is to be gotten out of these rogues. Zack flushes crimson, and just as he is about to get fierce, a cunning grin flashes across his scarred face. Despite their misleading statements, the four crooks have betrayed themselves.

Zack knows one thing for sure: none of these men is lying. He takes a piece of paper and draws the following diagram on it:

	Football	Movies	Harry's Hamburgers	Naschmarkt
Albert				
Burt				
Charlie				
Danny				

Zack lights up his pipe and thinks a while. (He can only think if he has paper, a pencil, and his pipe.) Soon he knows not only who was where at the time of the crime, but even more important, who was at the Naschmarkt.

Do you know who it was? (See: Solutions on p. 139.)

LUGER

A person who owns a Luger believes that with this piece of technology, he is more than a match for anyone. And he remains convinced of this fact until the day he himself eats lead.

WARNING: In the end, all guns backfire.

M

MA BARKER

Arizona Donnie Barker (1872–1935), called "Ma," lived in the American Midwest and was a law-abiding citizen and loving mother of four sons. In the late 1920s, at the age of 55, she left her husband and became a gangster boss.

Barker's life took this turn because she almost constantly needed money to get her wayward sons out of jail. Bail*, lawyers, and bribes cost money.

Barker knew only too well that her sons— Herman, Lloyd, Freddy, and Arthur, known as "Doc"—were much too dumb to successfully pull off a job themselves. So she decided to take charge. She organized and planned bank holdups and provided for clean getaways. When her plans were realized, she pocketed a fat portion of the cash.

Everything was going like clockwork. Even famous gangster bosses had Ma Barker work out schemes for them. And as long as the boys obeyed their mother, the Ma Barker Gang, also called the "Bloody Barkers," was swimming in money. Yet Ma's sons began to feel pampered, and so they took part—without her knowledge—in a badly organized **kidnapping** fiasco.

Barker's talent for playing the cops and robbers game kept the gang above water for a time. But then everything went wrong. Herman was the first to go. He shot himself when he was cornered by the Kansas City police. Then in 1935, Ma and her youngest son, Freddy, were pumped full of lead in a shoot-out with the **FBI.** Doc bit the dust when trying to break out of **Alcatraz.** Lloyd spent 25 years in prison, only to be killed by his wife shortly after his release.

* Money exchanged for the release of an arrested person as a guarantee of his or her appearance for trial.

MACDONALD, ROSS

This MacDonald has nothing to do with hamburgers, french fries, or other such delicacies. Ross MacDonald (1915–1983), whose real name was Kenneth Millar, is among the most distinguished American mystery writers. His hero, private detective Lew Archer, is a worthy successor to Philip Marlowe (see: **famous detectives**).

Some of MacDonald's many stories are *The Moving Target, The Drowning Pool, The Way Some People Die, The Far Side of the Dollar, Meet Me at the Morgue, The Underground Man,* and *The Chill.*

MAFIA

Many different criminal organizations exist, but the most well-known is the Mafia, or *La Cosa Nostra*. Originally a secret association in southern Italy, it protected its members from unjust rulers. In the 1880s, the Mafia was brought to the United States. These days the Mafia makes millions of dollars on drugs, gambling, and prostitution throughout the world. During the 1930s, battles between Mafia gangs were quite common (see: **Al Capone, gangsters**).

MAUSER

Pronounced like "mouse + r," it has nothing to do with the common gray rodent. Mauser is the favorite brand of handgun-crazy detectives. The slogan for this product reads: "To carry one is to know its value." In this advertisement, not a word is wasted on the senselessness of shooting someone dead.

WHAT? OH YEAH! I DECIDED TO TAKE ACTION —

AND RUSHED TO THE DOOR, BEHIND WHICH SOMEONE

WHEN I OPENED THE DOOR, I WAS BLINDED BY A BRIGHT LIGHT.

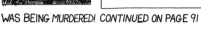

WAS BEING MURDERED! CONTINUED ON PAGE 91

MINI-MYSTERY

Two men shout.
One's knocked out.
The killer runs.
A cop draws guns.
"Hands in the air!"
Ending: fair.

MOTIVE

The murder victim: Johann S., bank employee, 53 years old, married, two adult children. *The cause of death:* **arsenic** in red wine.

For the detective investigating this crime, just about everyone is a possible suspect, especially everyone in the victim's circle of acquaintances: bank colleagues, drinking pals, business friends, circus directors, his nephew in England, his aunt in Africa, his barber, his neighbors, the mail carrier, the tailor, the gas station attendant, the mayor....

But is it possible for the detective to interrogate all the suspects in detail? No, it isn't. The detective's suspicions will be cast on those who had a motive—that is, those who had a reason to send Mr. Johann S. to his grave. Possibilities are:

Victoria, his wife
Her husband was known for gawking at
pretty girls.
Motive: jealousy

Marilyn, his daughter
Her father was a tyrant. She
wasn't allowed to stay out
after 8:00 P.M.
Motive: freedom

Jerry, his son
He will inherit the estate.
Motive: greed

Franz Joseph, business associate
He owed Johann S. money,
and payment was due soon.
Motive: short of cash

Evita P., the family's housekeeper
Johann S. had caught her stealing a roll of
toilet paper, and she feared being
reported to the police.
Motive: fear

Karl M., the family's postal
carrier
He didn't receive a present
at Christmas.
Motive: revenge

What do you think? Note: The existence of a motive alone does not make someone a murderer!

Just for fun, here's a small assignment to sharpen the junior detective's memory for faces: Who are or were the six persons pictured on the opposite page in real life? (See: Solutions on p. 140.)

MURDER INVESTIGATION

The sky was cloudy. Fog hung over the narrow streets, and a light mist filled the air. Suddenly, the flashing lights of a police car cut through the haze, and tires screeched to a halt. Criminal Inspector Fuet jumped out of the car, turned up the collar of his coat, pulled his hat down even farther, and entered the building at 41 Elm Street. The lights were on in the third-floor apartment, and the door was ajar. A police officer keeping watch led Fuet into the living room. There, on the carpet, lay the corpse. From a small round bullet hole in the forehead dripped a thin trickle of blood. Fuet pushed back his hat, lit a cigarette, and got down to work....

Many mystery novels begin in a similar fashion. Though there may be some truth to them, there is hardly a criminal inspector who would react so indifferently when confronted with a dead body. And when several murders take place, mysterious figures enter into the plot, and shots are fired in an ambush, the inspector gets into quite a jam. Yet, in the end—thanks to the inspector's keen perception and heroic efforts—the case is solved.

In reality, however, an investigation proceeds quite differently. Unromantically, and not at all mysteriously, a team of specialists and their assistants get down to work on the case.

First, the corpse is photographed from all sides, its position outlined on the floor and sketched.

Then the apartment is searched for **clues:** letters, address books, telephone messages, documents, not to mention the murder weapon, and any other articles that may turn out to provide important clues.

Fingerprints are taken from the weapon, doorknobs, glass-top tables, bottles, even the victim's eyeglasses, to be handed over to the department of criminal identification.

Empty cartridges, bullets in the walls, and the deadly one in the victim's body are examined by **weapons experts.** Such experts can determine whether and when a weapon was fired, from what angle and distance the shot was taken, and which bullet came from which gun.

Official medical experts examine the corpse. They are often able to establish the time and cause of death. They can determine what the victim ate for dinner and if the person had relieved himself afterward. They can also find out if a struggle took place before the murder and if the corpse had been moved (see: **autopsy**).

The officers from the forensics squad, who secure the clues, gather bloodstains, dirt on the carpet from muddy shoes, traces of lipstick on cigarette filters, a long black hair on the suit of the victim, as well as the dirt from under the corpse's fingernails. These clues are then analyzed by chemists.

Neighbors are questioned: Did someone go into the house at such and such a time? What did this person look like? How was he or she dressed? To which floor did the person go? Did you hear any shots? How many? When? Did the victim often receive guests at this hour? Who were the murdered person's friends and acquaintances? What kind of neighbor was the victim? Did one sometimes hear a quarrel in the apartment? What were the victim's habits? When? How? Where? Who? What? How long? How many? Why? (See: **seven golden questions**.) Friends, acquaintances, relatives, colleagues, and the housekeeper are all bombarded with questions in a similar manner.

Meanwhile, the chatty apartment manager talks the police officer's head off. A neighbor who does not want to be disturbed slams the door in his face. One tenant, a would-be detective, gives him good tips. An aunt of the victim casts suspicion on a cousin whom she does not like. The bragging bar owner tells more than he knows in order to play up his part.

The detective then has to record all of these interviews and write a report about each of them. Forms have to be filled out and papers signed. Documents are sealed and cataloged. Files are opened, copies made, holes punched, pages dog-eared, **spelling** errors corrected, and splotches of ink removed. And to think that there are junior detectives who believe that they don't have to learn how to spell!

This whole mountain of paperwork lands on the inspector's desk. It's no wonder that his pipe fumes, his typewriter quakes, and his brain almost short-circuits. Then he begins to put the small clues together, like the pieces of a puzzle. A picture begins to emerge. If parts are still missing, he gives the command for further interviews and investigations. The mountain of paperwork on

his desk grows another foot or two.

When he has a clear picture of what happened (that is, when enough **evidence** has been gathered), the detective can apply for a warrant for the suspect's arrest. If apprehended, the suspect is held in pretrial detention and the detective interrogates him. If the suspect confesses, the inspector can breathe freely again—the case is closed. But wait a second! First a final revision of the confession has to be drawn up, signed, and copied! The inspector then hands the suspect, and all the copies of the paperwork on his desk, over to the district attorney.

If the suspect does not make a confession, however, then.... No, never mind. Enough is enough!

What a wonderful life for the inspector in a novel. No case remains unsolved, and desks do not ever actually vanish under growing piles of papers.

...It had stopped raining, and the first rays of sunlight fell across his desk. Inspector Fuet leaned back contentedly, put his feet up on his desk, and lit a cigarette. Tomorrow he would take the train to Miami, lie in the sun on the beach, and enjoy some peace and quiet....

AS MY EYES
BEGAN TO
ADJUST TO
THE LIGHT,

I SAW...   I SAW...   I SAW...   CONTINUED ON PAGE 95

P

PICTOGRAMS

In some parts of the world, on the walls of old buildings and sheds, it is still possible to find mysteriously scribbled symbols— secret pictograms with which thieves and vagabonds communicated. Symbols like these are hardly used anymore, since the telephone, radio, and mail are more effective ways to send messages. Just the same, it is a good idea for modern detectives to be versed in a few of these symbols.

A pictogram found on the wall of a solitary chapel in a wooded area in Germany:

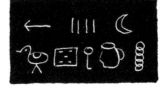

In the direction of ARROW, the FOURTH house will be broken into, on the night of the last quarter of the MOON. Underneath are the "signatures" of five crooks.

Pictograms found near a group of farm houses in the United States:

a)   b)   c)   d)   e)

a) Keep moving! Nothing to be had here.
b) Beware! Dog bites!
c) Alarm system!
d) Be courteous. This farm is run by women!
e) If you want something here, you have to work for it!

PINKERTON, ALLAN

In 1850 a Scottish immigrant named Allan Pinkerton (1819–1884) founded America's most famous detective agency. Pinkerton started the agency in Chicago, and within a few years he had opened branches in several cities. Pinkerton's agents, known as "Pinkerton men," operated throughout North America and were much feared because of their competence and ruthlessness.

During the Civil War (1861–1865), Pinkerton and his agents nabbed Rose Greenhow, a Confederate spy, and in 1868 they captured the Reno brothers, a gang of train robbers. Dashiell **Hammett** was once a Pinkerton detective.

Symbol and motto of the Pinkerton agency

POE, EDGAR ALLAN

Edgar Allan Poe (1809–1848) was a writer of poetry, horror, and mystery stories. His short story "The Murders in the Rue Morgue" (1841) is considered the first modern detective story, and Poe created the amateur detective Auguste Dupin (see: **famous detectives**). Poe's other famous works include the stories "The Telltale Heart" and "The Cask of Amontillado," as well as the classic poem "The Raven."

Warning: Poe's writings are not recommended for use as bedtime stories!!!

POISON

Murder by poisoning is not very common, except in detective novels. Some of the poisons often used by murderers are:

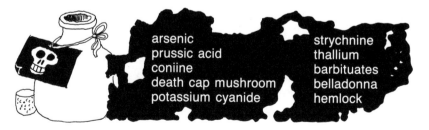

arsenic
prussic acid
coniine
death cap mushroom
potassium cyanide

strychnine
thallium
barbituates
belladonna
hemlock

Since these poisons are not easily bought at the local grocery store, a detective's suspicions are directed mainly toward people who have access to such poisons: doctors, nurses, pharmacists,

chemists, soldiers (poisonous gases), dentists, laboratory assistants, gardeners and farmers (insecticides), homemakers and warehouse workers (rat poison), drugstore employees, snake breeders, dry cleaners (chemical cleaning fluids), food manufacturers (chemical additives), drivers (poisonous emissions), mushroom hunters, and herbalists.

Toxicologists are trained experts in matters of poisoning. They know the nature and effects of poisons, and they can detect which poison has caused the untimely and often agonizing death.

POLICE DOGS

It's dark outside. A man in a tattered coat quickly turns a corner. Suddenly, he stops—rooted to the spot. He sees a police officer and a dog, ten steps ahead. The man whips out a gun from beneath his coat and takes aim. Dropping the leash, the officer gives a sharp word of command to the German shepherd at his side. The dog leaps at the man, and, with a growl, bites firmly into the man's arm, pulls him down, and pins him there. The shot the man fires misses its mark.

Another command from the officer and the dog lets go. It struts back to its master, while the man on the ground gets up grinning. He takes off his coat and unbuckles the leather pads lining the arms.

"Good work, friend!" he remarks approvingly, and praises the German shepherd as well. The dog has just passed lesson #76 in its training as a police dog.

Spotty, the mutt next door, has been attending dog school, and when he is in the mood, he understands "Sit!" "Heel!" and when to give his paw for a handshake. He is, however, a beginner compared to those who have graduated from the School of Higher Education for Police Dogs.

Four-legged detectives are rigorously trained and are just as specialized as their two-legged colleagues. Some dogs become sleuthhounds, and others train to be guard or tracking dogs.

A police dog will go through a line of gunfire for its master. It tracks down explosives and narcotics with its keen sense of smell, and picks up the invisible trails of fugitives. It's the dog's nose that is irreplaceable—neither human nor machine can approach its efficiency.

CONTINUED ON PAGE 104

PURSUIT

THE PURSUED CRIMINAL

(armed robber Joe F.)

Drat! Why did I have to go and knock off that money carrier? *Why* did I pull out my gun and blast away at him when he didn't turn over the cash? Where did it get me? Nowhere. Only a few lousy dollars, which aren't enough to help me much. Now, instead of lying under a palm tree in the hot Florida sand, I'm squatting here in this windy, dirty mountain hut. My clothes are soaked and I'm freezing. I don't dare make a fire, because the smoke would give me away. I'm starving. It's been days since I've had anything warm in my stomach. I'd pay half the loot for a hot cup of coffee.

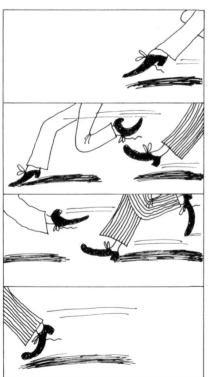

A wanted poster with my picture on it is hanging in every lousy post office and police station in the country. They've put a price on my head. The cops are working overtime. My description was broadcast on TV. My picture's in all the papers. Every punk kid who sees me will recognize me and run to the nearest police station. "Careful, he's armed!" Ridiculous! My hands are frozen stiff and I can't even bend a finger.

Should I run farther—over the mountains, over the border? How? My ankle is sprained and swollen. The blister on my heel has broken, and it's bloody and infected. It's foggy outside. I don't know the area, and I'd never find the way. And this lousy rain just won't stop. The cops from the border patrol are just waiting to pounce on me, their rifles cocked. They must have tracking dogs, too. And anyway, I'm beat! I haven't slept for two nights and it's too cold! With these skimpy wet rags on, it's pure suicide to go any farther. To heck with it! What can I do anyway? There's no way out....

THE PURSUER
(Criminal Inspector Frank Z.)

Drat! The search has been going full force for three days, and still no trace of that killer! He's probably already lying under a palm tree in the hot Florida sand, loot and all. I wish I could do the same. I haven't slept in three nights. I've had to run the whole search on six pots of coffee. What good are all the wanted posters, announcements on TV, and the photos in the papers? The guy's probably shaved off his beard, dyed his hair, and changed his clothes. Everyone is looking for a dark blue turtleneck pullover and black corduroy pants, while he's probably running around in a gray striped suit and a yellow tie.

Yeah, sure. My people are posted at all the train stations, airports, and freeway exits. The border patrol has been notified and **Interpol** informed. But it's so easy for someone to slip through the crowds these days! And anyway, with money, anything's possible. And he has money.

Sure, sure. The homes of his friends, family, and acquaintances—they're all under close surveillance. My detectives are standing around pretending to read newspapers in the lobbies of all the big hotels. But I can't have every house in the country watched.

And what if he's gone over the mountains? With this fog, he can slip through the tightest of nets. And the net up there in the mountains isn't all that tight. Personnel shortages up there as well. Tracking dogs are useless in this rainy weather.

It was a mistake to offer a reward. Every Tom, Dick, and Suzy wants to cash in on it. Over 200 calls in the past three days, and all of them dead ends or false alarms. My officers have followed every lead. Nothing has come of any of them. No wonder they're only halfhearted about this case.

With every day that passes, the odds of catching this scoundrel are more and more against us. Newer warrants have been issued and the older ones end up in the file. I don't think it's possible. How are we ever going to catch him...?

Q

QUEEN, ELLERY

With the pen name Ellery Queen, a team of two mystery writers concealed their true identities: Frederic Dannay (1905–1982) and Manfred B. Lee (1905–1971), cousins from New York City. In their youth, they entered a detective story competition and won first prize. They wrote over 40 suspenseful thrillers, and they founded

Ellery Queen's Mystery Magazine in 1941. The detective in their stories is called Ellery Queen as well. For children, Dannay and Lee also created the young detective Milo Trbuchovitch (see: **famous detectives**).

Frederic Dannay

Manfred B. Lee

S

SAYERS, DOROTHY

Dorothy Leigh Sayers (1893–1957) was an English writer, born in Oxford, who had an extreme talent for making our blood curdle. In Sayers's mysteries, the well-bred and dignified detective Lord Peter Wimsey (see: **famous detectives**) wages a valiant fight against crime. Sayers dropped Lord Wimsey after having made a mint off him in 11 books. She then wrote exclusively religious and philosophical works, and spent the last years of her life translating Dante's *Divine Comedy* from Italian into English.

SCENE OF THE CRIME—TIME OF THE CRIME

SCENE OF THE CRIME

The elderly duchess was dead. Murdered. And it was plain that the cook had murdered her. Though the cook lamented and pleaded her innocence, it wouldn't do her a bit of good—the **evidence** was totally against her. She was the only person present at the scene of the crime (the duchess's bedroom) at the time of the crime. The murder weapon—a heavy silver ladle—lay next to the victim. The cook's fingerprints were all over the bedroom. It was a clear case. The cook had done it.

Criminal Inspector Zack and his staff were, however, prudent and thorough workers. The mud on the duchess's clothing, the tiny pieces of grass in the deadly wound, and the pine needles in the hem of her skirt all indicated that the place where the corpse was discovered (the bedroom) was not, in fact, the scene of the crime. Instead, the duchess must have been murdered somewhere in the garden. After further investigation, the detectives found the true scene of the crime and arrested the gardener, whose fingerprints matched those on the silver ladle. He had killed the duchess in a hidden corner of the garden and dragged her to the bedroom, casting suspicion on the cook. A classic frame-up!

| THE GARDENER | CRIMINAL INSPECTOR ZACK | THE COOK |

TIME OF THE CRIME

The elderly duchess was dead. And it was plain that the gardener had murdered her. He lamented and pleaded his innocence, but it wouldn't do him a bit of good—the evidence was totally against him. There were footprints from his boots at the scene of the crime, and his fingerprints were on the weapon. Moreover, when the duchess was killed, her wristwatch had been smashed and had stopped working—at 3:04 P.M., the exact time of the crime. It was a clear case. The gardener had done it.

Criminal Inspector Zack and his staff were, however, prudent and thorough workers. According to the results of the **autopsy,** the time of the crime was 1:00 P.M. Further investigation proved that the watch had been smashed by the murderer after the killing and set at 3:04 P.M., a time that would incriminate the gardener. It could be proven that at the actual time of the crime (1:00 P.M.), he had not been in the garden. The murderer was, of course, the cook. Wearing the gardener's boots, she had dragged the corpse into the bedroom, apparently to cast suspicion on herself. Yet she had known that the police would see through such a blatant frame-up, and that they would then suspect the gardener (a double frame-up).

After this complicated case, Inspector Zack spent weeks in a psychiatric hospital. He was, at times, quite delirious, and he could be heard mumbling, ''...time of the crime, time of the scene, local time, local crime, local time crime, scene of the crime time, time of the scene of the crime, crime of the time crime, time of the crime time, scene of the crime crime, time of the crime scene....''

SCOTLAND YARD

OLD SCOTLAND YARD

London's Scotland Yard is the most famous police headquarters in the world. It's not famous because it possesses criminological research laboratories, a huge file of **fingerprints,** and an archive on criminals. Nor is it particularly famous for its crime museum called the "Black Museum," nor because it employs approximately 30,000 police officers. Many other police headquarters around the world can boast of the same. Scotland Yard is famous due to all the mystery stories that have come from England. The detectives in these stories usually have to work with Scotland Yard—it's as simple as that.

The mounties from the Royal Canadian Mounted Police (RCMP), the federales from the Federale of Mexico, the flics from the Prefecture de Police in Paris, the cops from the **FBI** in Washington, the Bullen of the Bundeskrimnalamt in Wiesbaden, and the Kieberer from the Bundespolizeidirektion in Vienna are, of course, just as industrious as their legendary colleagues in London.

SEARCH WARRANT

A detective or police officer cannot enter the apartment or house of a suspect and rummage around looking for **evidence** without permission. The detective or officer needs a search warrant, a written order issued by a magistrate (a kind of judge), which then has to be presented to the occupant of the apartment or house upon entrance. It is only then that the detective can turn everything upside down.

While the warrant was being written and approved, however, the suspect may have gotten rid of the murder weapon, incriminating letters, and bloodstained clothes and shoes. And the detective usually messes up everything for nothing.

For a more profitable search, experienced detectives sometimes wear a **disguise** that allows them to enter the suspect's house unnoticed. Dressed as a chimney sweep, an electrician, a baby-sitter, or a plumber, the detective will sneak into the house and search clogged drains, hollow toilet seats, rolling pins with secret compartments, and camouflaged mouse holes for valuable **clues.**

SECRET AGENTS

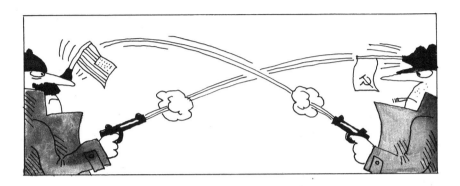

To be truthful, secret agents, or spies, do not have much in common with detectives, other than that they both pull their hats down low and turn their collars up. What little we know about them we have learned mostly from novels and films. Here is a typical plot:

Secret Agent 0003's boss, 0001, gives him the assignment to infiltrate enemy country X, to make contact with go-between 040 in order to eliminate the dreaded enemy BX365. With the assistance of Agent 6, 0003 is able to swipe the plans for a new kind of super weapon or military secret. The whole mission is given the code name "Operation C3D8 Violet-Blue."

So far, everything is as clear as day. Now for the complicated part: Go-between 040 is in fact not 040, but 216c of the counterorganization 3-44-2; BX365 is a double agent and 6 is an alias for $*814^2$. $(x - y)$ is r^2II, while $2rII$ is in fact 9. H^2, who is supposed to be liquidated by 6,783754%, is mistaken for $\frac{7}{8}$ and knocked off by the treacherous $816m^2$. Yet despite all the mix-ups, Agent 0003 slips through the finely spun enemy defense network, avoiding all traps and attempts on his life, and extracts the cubic roots of a few nasty numbers in the process.

Blood-spattered, with one eye gouged out, 17 teeth missing, and an ugly spot of red wine on his tie, Agent 0003 hands over the desired documents to 0001. Agent 0001 bawls him out for his appearance, but still gives him the OK for a three-day vacation in Miami.

Though spy novels and films probably have little to do with reality, secret services do exist. The United States has its CIA (Central Intelligence Agency); the Soviet Union had, until 1991, its KGB (*Komitet Gosudarstvennoi Bezopastnost'i*, or Committee of State Security); and during the Second World War, Nazis formed the notorious Gestapo (*Geheime Staatspolizei*, or Secret National Police) in Germany.

These days, military information is often acquired by way of aerial photos taken from reconnaissance satellites. We sometimes hear about diplomats and other embassy employees who are involved in espionage and actually expelled from countries. But we don't know much more about them. Most likely, the only people who know what life in the secret services is really like are those who are involved—and they are required to keep quiet.

WHEN I TAKE ACTION, I MEAN BUSINESS!

I RUSHED AT THE FIEND AND KNOCKED HIM OUT COLD.

CONTINUED ON PAGE 109

SECRET CODES

The famous detective Auguste Dupin (see: **famous detectives**) was sitting at his desk and staring at a sheet of paper:

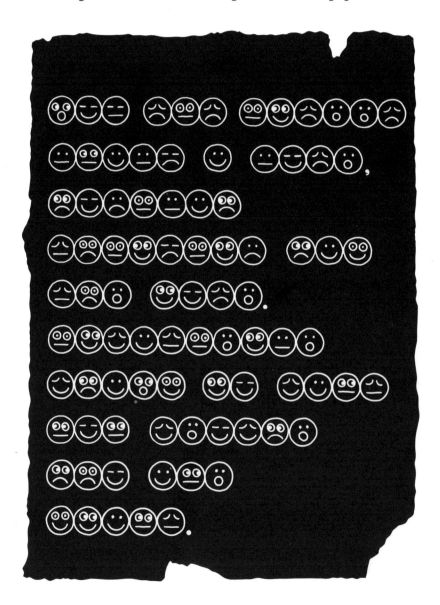

Dupin had received the paper from an Australian colleague, who had found it when searching a suspect's apartment (see: **search warrant**). The colleague hadn't been able to make heads or tails of it, and even Dupin thought at first that it was merely a doodle—a child's drawing perhaps, or something similar. Yet after looking at it more closely, he suspected and then knew for certain that it was a message written in a secret code.

Dupin got down to work immediately. He pondered, analyzed, and checked, until at last he found the solution! He had worked it out singlehandedly, by following these principles:

1. There is no secret code that can't be deciphered.
2. Each symbol represents a letter. Therefore, identical symbols represent the same letter.
3. Words are separated by spaces on each side.
4. The message is written in English.
5. Among the most commonly used letters in the English language are the letters *E, A, O, I,* and *D.* (Using this information, one can count the number of identical symbols in the message, assign the letters *E, A, O, I,* and *D* to the most common of them, and fill in these letters where they occur in the message.) Other most commonly used letters are *T, N, R, S,* and *H.*
6. The message can then be worked out step-by-step, beginning with the words that have been largely filled in with letters—a little guesswork is involved here.
7. Each new letter discovered is entered into the rest of the text.
8. Patience, patience, patience, patience, patience, and more patience!

WARNING: Only quick-witted master detectives with unlimited patience should tackle this task! (May cause brains to scramble.) (See: Solutions on p. 140.)

CAESAR'S KEY

All large police headquarters employ specialists for deciphering codes (called decoding or crypt analysis). Computers also provide assistance, and even complicated codes can often be cracked quickly.

The Roman general Julius Caesar used a system of encoding messages that moved each letter of the alphabet three places. In this code, the order of the letters themselves is not changed, making this cryptogram easy to decipher.

Caesar's key, or set of instructions for the code, was a turnable disk. Instead, we shall use two sheets of 8½" x 11" graph paper. Turn the first sheet lengthwise, and write the alphabet twice along one line. On the second sheet, also turned lengthwise, write the alphabet once along the top edge. Place the second sheet on top of the first, so that the alphabet on the second sheet is directly under the alphabet on the first sheet.

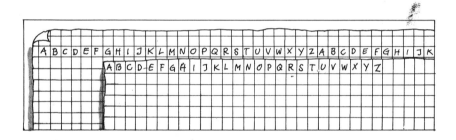

The first (bottom) sheet will represent the encoded letters, and the second (top sheet) will represent their decoded values. Move the second sheet far to the right, so that, for example, *A* is under *G*. The code letter *G* would then stand for *A*, and so on. So the following text in plain English

"WE ARE LEAVING TOMORROW EVENING"

turns into

"CK GXK RKGBOTM ZUSUXXUC KBKTOTM."

Here is a quite simple Code Cracker Program for computer-crazed junior detectives (suitable only for the "Caesar's key" described above):

```
100 REM DECODING OF "CAESAR-CODE"
110 REM THIS VERSION IS WRITTEN IN
    IBM-PC BASIC
120 REM COPYRIGHT BY W. ZWANGSLEITNER,
    14.1.1987
130 CLS: CLEAR
140 INPUT "ENCODED TEXT WITHOUT SPACES", T$
150 DIM Z(26)
160 FOR I=1 to LEN(T$)
170 NR=ASC(MID$(T$,I,1))-64
180 Z(NR)=Z(NR)+1
190 NEXT I
200 MAX=0
210 FOR I=1 TO 26
220 IF Z(I)>MAX THEN MAX=Z(I):NUM(I)
230 NEXT I
240 IF MAX=0 THEN PRINT "TEXT CONTAINS NO 'E'
    NO SOLUTION POSSIBLE"
250 VER=NUM-5
260 PRINT: PRINT
270 PRINT "TRIAL SOLUTION:": PRINT
280 FOR I=1 TO LEN(T$)
290 NR=ASC(MID$(T$,I,1))-VER: IF NR<65
    THEN NR=NR+26
300 PRINT CHR$(NR)
```

```
310 NEXT I
320 PRINT
330 INPUT "SOLUTION CORRECT (Y/N)",I$
340 IF I$<>"Y" THEN GOTO 360
350 END
360 Z(NUM)=0
370 GOTO 200
```

In line 140, the computer asks to be fed the coded text (without spaces!). In lines 160 to 230, the computer finds the most frequent symbol and assumes that it is an *E*. Based on this assumption, the program determines the number of spaces the alphabet has been shifted and prints out the solution (lines 250 and following).

Given the example "CKGXKRKGBOTMZUSUXXUCKBK-TOTM", the computer provides the correct solution on the first round ("WE ARE LEAVING TOMORROW EVENING").

However, if the input had been merely "RKGBOTMZUSUXX-UC" (LEAVING TOMORROW) the first solution would have read "BUQLYDWJECEHHEM." We would reject this answer, so the computer would erase the presumed *E* and replace it with the next most frequent letter of the sample, and so on, until we were satisfied with its solution.

In this example ("RKGBOTMZUSUXXUC"), the third solution the computer suggests will be the correct one. If we were to feed in only "ZUSUXXUC"—"TOMORROW," which contains no *E*, the computer would fail to find any solution at all. (See line 240—this is easy to adjust.)

For decoding longer messages, the speed of this program can't be beat. Even if *E* is not the most frequent letter used in the secret message, one single *E* is enough for the computer to eventually find the solution.

FOR LACK OF SPACE, PLEASE SEE PAGE 120

SEVEN GOLDEN QUESTIONS

When experienced detectives discover a crime, seven golden questions fly through their heads. They take out their notebooks and systematically ask:

Who are the victim, witness, and suspect?
What happened?
Where did it happen? In the forest? In an apartment? Somewhere else? (See: **scene of the crime**.)
With what kind of weapon was the crime committed?
How? And if possible, in detail.
When? (See: **scene of the crime**.)
Why? (See: **motive**.)

Detectives should never even consider the question, **how much?** (See: **bribery**.)

SIMENON, GEORGES

Georges Simenon was a Belgian mystery writer who wrote over 200 novels. He created Inspector Maigret (see: **famous detectives**).

Faster than Maigret could solve his cases, Simenon wrote them. At the rate of 80 typewritten pages a day, he could finish a book in 8 to 10 days.

SING SING

...although the inmates of New York's most famous prison have absolutely no reason to do so. For them, the prison should be called "Sob Sob" or "Sigh Sigh."

All over the world, prisoners are drawn wearing black-and-white pajamalike suits. But actually, this fashionable outfit is worn only by inmates of Sing Sing. The prisoners probably like the suit—an escaped prisoner on the run could stop to catch his breath at a masquerade party.

SKELETON KEY

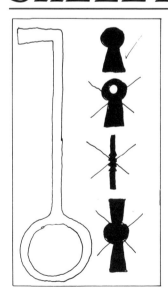

Locked doors are not only a hindrance for thieves and burglars, but for detectives as well. With a skeleton key, (also called a master key, passkey, picklock, or passe-partout), a bit of dexterity, and some luck, a detective can pick a simple lock. When held at a downward angle, the skeleton key hooks into the keyhole; when it's straightened and carefully turned to the right, the catch bolt can then be slid or withdrawn.

When it comes to safety locks, dead bolts, or combination locks, a skeleton key is at best useful for perplexedly picking one's nose.

Here's one detective's method for opening locked doors without a skeleton key:

SLANG

The above example clearly illustrates how important it is to use
the proper language when dealing with criminals. Fashionable
around the world is a somewhat coolly spoken slang. With a touch
of slightly dry humor, it indicates to even the most cold-blooded
gangster bosses that you mean business. Cultivated Standard
English will, at best, earn a detective a few loud guffaws.

The gangster slang listed below can be expanded by the language-oriented junior detective. And since the modern detective of to-day is quite international, slang from several languages has been included. Naturally, this list should be adapted to the detective's local area of operation, since the language habits of criminals in Chicago, Los Angeles, Miami, New York, London, Hong Kong, Marseille, Bangkok, Rio, Bogotá, and _____ * do vary slightly.

*Your hometown.

SLANG	**STANDARD ENGLISH**
(G = German, S = Spanish, F = French, I = Italian)	
beanshooter, rod, piece; (G) Knarre, Puffer; (F) un flingue	gun, revolver
beat it! scram! shove off! (G) Schleich dich! Hau ab! (S) vete! lárgate! arranca! fuera! (F) taille-toi! casse-toi! dégage!; (I) vattene!	go away! leave!
belt, clobber, bash, bonk, wallop; (G) fotzen, vermöbeln; (S) dar una torta; (F) latter, amocher, bastonner, casser la gueule; (I) ti spacco la faccia	beat up, deliver a blow with the fist
bloke, cat, dude; (G) Kerl, Typ; (S) un tío; (F) un keum, le type, le mec; (I) un tipo	man, fellow
booze, juice, tiger's milk, medicine; (G) Alk, Oel; (F) bibine; (I) benzina	alcohol, liquor

sloshed, bombed, hammered; (G) fett, breit; (S) borracho; (F) avoir un coup dans le nez; (I) brillo, fare il pieno	drunk, intoxicated
bread, dough, spinach, cabbage; (G) Kies, Marie, Knete, Kohle; (S) chibilines, pasta; (F) le fric; (I) i quattrini	money
buck, greenback, lettuce; (F) un petit vert	dollar
bump off, rub out, off, polish off; (G) umlegen, hamdrahn; (S) mandar al otro mundo; (F) envoyer six pieds sous terre, buter; (I) spedire due metri sotto terra	kill, murder
slammer, clink, jug, can, coop, cooler, joint; (G) Knast, Häfen; (S) la cana; (F) la tôle, le trou; (I) la gattabuia	prison
choppers, china, ivories, fangs; (G) Beisser, Stockerln, Hauer; (F) les quenottes; (I) le zanne	teeth
chow, eats, grub; (G) Fressen; (S) combo; (F) la bouffe	food
punk, bum, runt, pip-squeak, small potato; (G) Penner, Knirps, ein kleiner Fisch; (S) el chorizo, don nadie; (F) un zonard, une petite frappe; (I) un perdigiorno, un ceffo	an unimportant person or nobody, a petty criminal

cop, rip off, lift, boost, pinch, bag; (G) klauen, fladern; (S) mangar; (F) chouraver, tirer, taxer, braquer; (I) fregare	steal
dick, flatfoot, gumshoe, Sweeny; (G) Schnüffler, Kieberer; (S) el sabueso; (F) un privé	detective
eat lead; (G) abgeknallt werden; (S) se lo bajaron, alcanzar; (F) se faire descendre, se faire buter; (I) mangiare il piombo	get hit by bullets
five finger, filcher, looter; (G) Fladerer, Langfinger; (S) el chorizo; (F) un taxeur; (I) svelto di mano	thief
freeze!; (I) ferma o sparo!	don't move!
wheels, heap, tub, crate; (G) Kiste, Kübel, Karre; (F) une caisse, une bagnole	car
gut, breadbasket, paunch; (G) Wampe, Gössermuskel; (S) la barriga; (F) le bide; (I) il buzzo	stomach, belly
hit the road, split, make tracks, skip town, fly the coop; (G) die Platte putzen, abseilen; (S) largarse; (F) se tailler, se barrer; (I) tagliare la corda	leave, depart, escape
hot seat, chair	electric chair
ice, rock; (G) Glitzermurrer, Klunker; (F) les joubis, diams; (I) la pietra	diamond, gem, jewels

joint, dive, hole; (G) Kneipe, Beisel; (F) un troquet, un rade; (I) una bettola	bar, pub, meeting place
lollipop, jellyfish, chicken, yellow-belly, fraidy-cat; (G) Schisser, Seicherl; (S) la gallina; (F) un dégonflé, un flan, un trouillard	cowardly person
noodlehead, nincompoop, nitwit, lamebrain, meathead; (G) Trottel, Pfeife; (S) tonto; (F) un cave, un connard; (I) un suonato	dumb person, idiot
paddy wagon, meat wagon; (G) Wanne; (F) panier à salade	police car or van
paws, mitts, meathooks; (G) Pfoten, Pratzen; (S) las patas; (F) les paluches, les battoirs; (I) zampe	hands
copper, fuzz, boys in blue; (G) Bulle, Schanti, Polente; (F) les flics, les keufs; (I) la madama caramba	police officer, police
sing, squeal, fink, rat, snitch; (G) verpfeifen, singen; (S) cantar; (F) moucharder, cafter; (I) cantare	inform on, betray
zap, drop, pump full of lead; (S) herir a alguien; (F) cartoner; (I) bucare	shoot at
cig, butt, cancer stick; (G) Kippe, Fluppe, Tschick; (S) fallo; (F) une clope, une tige; (I) una cicca	cigarette

kisser, mug;   face
  (G) Birne, Plutzer;
  (S) la caratula, la jeta;
  (F) la tronche; (I) il muso

For junior detectives with the right touch: translate the comic strip below into Standard English. (See: Solutions on p. 140.)

SMITH-WESSON

With just one shot from a Smith-Wesson Model 547, you can silence a person permanently. Whether or not you enjoy the peace and quiet afterward is quite another matter.

SPELLING

You don't think this subject has anything to do with detectives? Think again, after you've read the sad story of poor speller Detective S.:

(See: Solutions on p. 141.)

STOOL PIGEON

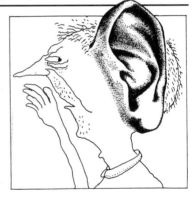

Carl B.'s life is truly dismal. He hangs out in the most disreputable bars and fills himself up with cheap booze. In earlier days, he was the famous Longfinger Charley—a respected pickpocket in his world. But eight years in the cooler have done him in. No, he doesn't want to go back to prison. No more crooked tricks, he has promised himself. But with his record, he can't find a job. And anyway, in that "other" world, the "straight," law-abiding world, he doesn't know his way around. He grew up here in the seedy milieu of the underworld. His friends are here, and this is where he understands what makes people tick.

But how does he make a living? Where does he get the money to eat and keep a roof over his head? He has a job, and all he has to do is to prick up his ears. He finds out about all sorts of things: the hideouts of wanted criminals, planned bank robberies, where the loot is stashed, and who broke into the warehouse. He then sells this information to the police. He doesn't get much for it— just enough to buy his next bottle of cheap gin.

Members of the underworld look down on him, because he no longer takes part in their activities. They are also slowly becoming suspicious. When Carl is nearby, crooks are careful to keep their voices low. The police have already gotten wise to too many of their schemes. Pity on Carl if the crooks figure out what he's up to! They'll beat him to a pulp, if not worse.

But the police aren't Carl's friends, either. To them he's merely a pickpocket, an ex-convict, a stool pigeon. "No information, no money!" the officers say. "Scram! And bring some useful information next time!"

Fellows like Carl are given all sorts of names—from stool pigeon to squealer, tattletale, blabber, and fink. Sometimes they are called informants, or "the source," but the title doesn't alter their reputations. These half-detective, half-gangster individuals usually lead very lonely lives.

T

TAILING

Commander Toothbury was in an extremely bad mood. He was seated at his desk, his fists clenched on top of a stack of files. At a respectful distance, three detectives from his department stood in front of him, their eyes shifting from floor to ceiling, their fingers fidgeting nervously.

"So, gentlemen," Toothbury barked, "there's no way we can go on like this. For days now we've been just about dead sure that Danny O'Tool blew the safe at the Crab & Junk Company. But we need evidence! EVIDENCE, gentlemen! And worst of all, we don't know where he's stashed the loot."

The commander paused and straightened the files. There was an awkward silence.

"Jones, Smith, and Wesson," he continued, "you're all going to do something for your health."

Jones became even paler than he already was, Smith tried to pull in his bulging belly, and Wesson shifted his weight from one foot to the other—from his flatfooted left foot to his right with the fallen arch.

"Exercise is healthy. Especially long walks. You are going to tail O'Tool till we've got evidence in our hands and know where he's hidden the contents of the safe. Gentlemen you're dismissed!"

Jones, Smith, and Wesson left the room, dragging their feet. Walks! Very funny indeed!

Tailing means keeping on the suspect's heels for miles, not losing sight of him or her for even a second, *and* remaining invisible in the process.

Tailing means waiting around for hours in the rain, your toes numb from the cold, and so tired you can hardly keep your eyelids up.

Tailing means hastily gulping down a sandwich, leaving behind an unfinished cup of coffee, and not being able to take a bathroom break when you need to.

And if you turn your head, you can lose the person: in a crowd, in the subway, in a taxi, or in a back alley with a secret exit. And when the suspect gets wise to being tailed, he or she stays home and drinks hot tea. The detectives wait outside, and wait some more, until they are mere shadows of their former selves.

No, tailing is not the same as going for a walk.

A common system of tailing is the "ABC system." Here's the trick:

The three detectives alternate their positions constantly so that they won't be recognized. One of them is positioned on the opposite side of the street so that the distance between the detectives and the suspect does not become too wide. For example, the suspect might suddenly cross the street on a red light. But a law-abiding detective wouldn't take such a risk, so his or her partner on the other side would keep up with the suspect.

Starting positions: A and B follow the suspect; C is on the other side.

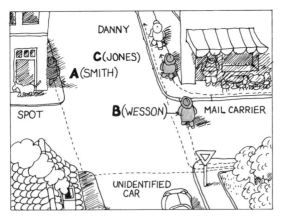

After a turn to the right: A is now opposite the suspect, C, and B.

By the way, Jones, Smith, and Wesson were successful in tailing Danny. Plus, Wesson's orthopedist made a few extra bucks, Smith's belly disappeared, and with a cold and a temperature of 101°F, Jones's face took on a more-than-healthy glow.

IT'S QUITE EMBARRASSING (TO BE STARED AT (BY HUNDREDS OF THEATER-*GOERS!* (ONCE AGAIN I TOOK ACTION...

CONTINUED ON PAGE 126

TERRORISM

By definition, a terrorist is someone who uses terror, usually by acts of violence, to achieve a political goal. Terrorists fight for the release of political prisoners, human rights, or to bring the downfall of a government. They use various means: planting bombs, hijacking airplanes, kidnapping, or assassinating politicians.

Measures taken to combat terrorism include the deployment of the secret services and anti-terrorist commandos, as well as retaliation. The consequences of dealing with terrorism are often discouraging: more blood and more deaths.

The politically alert junior detective knows that protesters who stage sit-ins or marches are often labeled "terrorists" by their opponents. For this reason, terrorism should not be viewed through glasses of the black-and-white variety.

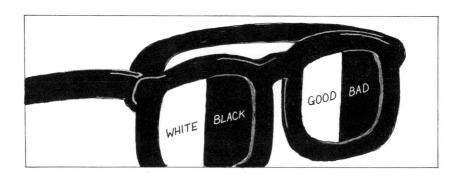

TRAINING PROGRAMS FOR DETECTIVES

So how do people become detectives? First they must have their high school diplomas. Then, to become inspectors or commissioners, they must complete courses at a university law school. At this point, future detectives may find a job in a criminal investigation department, but they still must take courses in criminology, forensic medicine, psychology, penal law, criminal procedure, police and civil service law, communications, weapons training, and self-defense. And even after having met all these qualifications, they aren't given a breather. Detectives must continuously broaden their education through advanced courses and specialist training. The **FBI,** for example, requires its agents to attend the National Police Academy at Quantico, Virginia, in addition to having a university degree. The FBI also demands that new agents be between 23 and 35 years of age and American citizens.

Does anyone still feel like becoming a detective? For those of you who would be satisfied with becoming something less than a commissioner, there are other, less demanding possibilities. But all detectives—from the simple cop on the beat to the head of **Interpol**—have to do their homework.

Teacher (strict) | Participates well, but wobbles around in his chair | Has to stand in the corner for not waiting his turn

V

VIDOCQ, FRANÇOIS E.

François Vidocq is often called the "Father of Criminal Science," or the "first detective." But wait a second—the systematic junior detective who is fond of order asks—why wasn't he listed under the **famous detectives** entry? It's a good question.

The reason is that that entry included only fictitious heroes. François Vidocq, however, was a real person, of flesh and blood, who lived in France about 200 years ago. It was the time of the French Revolution and of Napoleon, a rough period—but Vidocq was even rougher.

He grew up in a town in the north of France. His playmates were, for the most part, children of scoundrels, and he loved a good street brawl. Without ever having attended school, he learned several foreign languages and how to fence, read, write, and do arithmetic.

When at the age of 14 he ran away from home, one adventure followed the next. He got mixed up with bad company, and, although he hadn't commited any crime, he landed in prison. He escaped and was then pursued and hunted down, and sent back to prison. Once again he escaped, and this went on and on. Neither chains nor dungeons could stop him, and Vidocq was able to flee from the police 25 times in all.

Vidocq became famous—not only with the police, but also in the criminal underworld. He was never involved in a crime. But he got to know the customs and dirty tricks of the underworld like the back of his hand. He was hated by the police and worshipped by criminals.

At the age of 34, Vidocq had had enough of life on the run. He turned himself over to the police. One imagines that the police chief was speechless when Vidocq declared that he wanted to become a detective and help the police. But the police chief accepted Vidocq's proposal, and the master of escape became a chief detective in Paris. The hunted man became the hunter.

Does this sound strange? It wouldn't if you knew what the police system was like in those days. Police officers wore cheerfully colored uniforms, marched briskly in time, their sabres clattering. Quite impressive, but not that effective in catching criminals. These were better times for the underworld. But Vidocq changed all this.

Vidocq founded the "Sûreté," or Security, the first detective department in the world. He sent out his officers—unshaven and in rags—to track down gangsters. For the first time ever, **clues** were secured and **evidence** was collected. Each case was looked at logically, the facts were combined and systematically ordered, and then the case was solved.

Vidocq's methods were enormously successful. Paris's criminal districts were gradually depopulated, and the prisons were filled. Vidocq's success received international acclaim. **Scotland Yard,** the **FBI,** and police departments all over the world were reorganized after the Sûreté model.

Vidocq's methods were also adopted by many detectives in novels. Even Sherlock Holmes did not hesitate to copy Vidocq—for François Vidocq was the master, the very first detective.

... AND TOOK OFF!   CONTINUED ON PAGE 135

W

WALLACE, EDGAR

Edgar Wallace (1875–1932) was an English novelist, journalist, and playwright. He was the first author to become wealthy by writing detective stories, in a true "rags-to-riches" career. He had grown up as a street urchin in the slums of London, and later died a wealthy man in Hollywood.

Wallace's books were sold to millions of people with the advertising slogan "It's impossible not to be gripped by Wallace." His most famous works of detective fiction are *The Fellowship of the Frog, Dark Eyes of London, The Green Archer, The Ringer, The Four Just Men,* and *The Squealer.* Wallace also co-wrote the script for the classic 1933 film *King Kong.*

WEAPONS EXPERTS

A woman loads a revolver, cocks it, coolly takes aim, and fires. Bam! The bullet hits its mark. But there is no painful scream, no spattering blood, no death rattle. The woman's target is a box stuffed with soft white cotton.

What is this woman doing? She is a weapons expert, or ballistics expert, and works for the police. She is shooting a gun that was found at the murder scene. She shoots into the cotton padding so that no marks or traces are left on the bullet, other than from the revolver barrel through which it passed. The bullet is then examined and compared to the bullet in the corpse. Through this procedure, the weapons expert can determine whether the revolver is in fact the murder weapon.

If the police identify a murder weapon, they have made considerable headway in solving a case. All firearms have a serial number, which is registered along with the name of the buyer when it's sold. So the detective can usually find out who bought a certain weapon. (This person is not necessarily the culprit, however, and the situation is much more complicated when the serial number has been filed off the gun, or when the gun has been purchased illegally or stolen.) An expert can also determine when the gun was last used.

It isn't common, of course, for a murderer to leave the murder weapon lying right next to the victim. But the fatal bullet is usually left at the scene—in the corpse. And it too can offer a weapons expert an astonishing amount of information.

By examining the bullet, the expert can determine which brand of gun it was fired from. From the **autopsy** results, the expert can determine the distance from which the victim was shot, and at what angle to the victim's body the gun was held.

A person who casually carries and shoots a revolver is not a weapons expert, but rather a gunman or gunwoman—and it surely won't be long before he or she is an expert on jails, too.

Based on the trace materials found on this bullet, famous weapons expert W. could determine the trajectory (path followed by the bullet) and solve this mysterious murder:

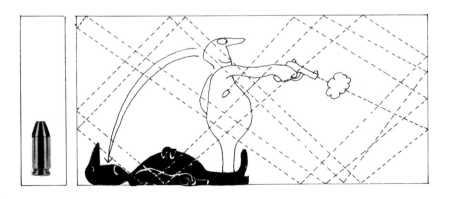

WHODUNNIT?

It was quiet in the lounge of London's Crime and Mystery Club. Bored, the members glanced through newspapers, ordered another round of whiskey, and puffed away at their cigars. Several members had already left and others were getting ready to go.

Then Inspector Brush arrived, and things livened up immediately. After greeting him respectfully, the Crime and Mystery Club members took seats at his table and eagerly waited for him to speak. Brush, known to his friends as "Comb," was always good for an exciting story.

As usual, Brush took his time. He leisurely lit his pipe, blew a few well-crafted smoke rings, leaned back in his chair, glanced with a smile around the circle, and then he began:

"Gentlemen, I'm sure you all expect me to tell you another tale in which I serve you the wrongdoer on a silver platter and you are all awed by my cleverness. I must disappoint you. This time you shall have to put your own minds to work and find the culprit yourselves."

An excited hum went through the group. "It is a matter," Brush continued, "of listening carefully and paying close attention to every detail." And he proceeded to tell the following tale:

Well, it was shortly after office hours, and not long after a tremendous thunderstorm, when I was called to Lord Benston's mansion.

"The family jewels," the Lord had gasped excitedly on the telephone, "are gone. Stolen! It's a scandal! Shocking!"

The large cast-iron gate to the estate was open, and I drove onto the grounds—over the pebbled driveway and up to the front of the house, which was brightly lit. A light drizzle was still falling, so the butler accompanied me with an umbrella up the steps into the house. Lord Benston was already in his nightclothes when he came to meet me, his face flaming red with indignation and his arms gesturing wildly.

"Thank goodness you've come, Inspector," he said, breathing heavily. "Let me tell you, it's just shocking, plain shocking...."

To make a long story short: the family jewels—valued at approximately 135,000 pounds—had been stolen, as had a small black case from the safe in Lord Benston's study. The crime had taken place at about 10:00 P.M.

Lord Benston babbled on while I examined the **scene of the crime.** The window in the study faced the back of the mansion. One shutter was open and a pane was smashed. Broken glass lay in the flower bed outside the window. The carpet was still wet where the rain had come in. The heavy door to the safe had been opened without force.

"Have you touched or moved anything?" I asked, interrupting his torrent of words.

"Of course not. Everything is as it was when we discovered the theft. The case with the jewelry lay here," whispered Lord Benston, pointing to the top compartment. "Luckily, it's insured."

"Who was here in the house this evening?" I asked.

"I, the butler, and the maid, Miss Tremble."

I questioned the maid first. She sat at the kitchen table and was quite shaken and frightened.

"Tell me what happened, Miss Tremble," I asked gently. She began hesitantly:

"You know, Inspector, sir, I have a terrible fear of thunderstorms. It was about 10:00, sir, when the storm was raging worst. I was just about to serve His Lordship a glass of sherry in his study, as I always do, sir."

Poor Miss Tremble sat anxiously gasping for air and wringing her hands in her apron.

"I was shaking so badly that I could hardly hold the tray. All of a sudden, I heard something shatter in the study. I was so startled that I spilled the sherry, sir. I thought that the storm had broken a window."

A pause. I helped her along: "You then rushed in to see what had happened?"

"No, not right away," she confessed. "It was a few minutes later, sir. And what a mess! Oh my! I ran straight to Mr. Banter, he's our butler, sir, and told him about it."

The butler, who had heard our conversation, was completely calm.

"Yes," he confirmed with a deep bass voice, "she came dashing up to me, and she was so out of breath that she couldn't get a word out. I was just taking off my galoshes and raincoat—I had been out by the garage, putting the car away."

"You ran past the broken window?" I asked him.

"Yes…" he drawled, "but at that point it was still in one piece. If you'll allow me the liberty, sir, there seemed to be someone in the room. I saw a shadow dart by the window. I'm not sure, however. I was, so to speak, tucked in deep in my raincoat and in a hurry to get back into the house."

With this comment, his account ended, and to the rest of my questions the butler merely shook his head in the negative. He had neither seen nor heard anything else.

In the distance, there was a clap of thunder. Lord Benston took me aside and remarked quite confidentially: "I believe, Inspector, you're on the wrong track. I would have put my hand in fire for Mr. Banter and Miss Tremble. They have been with me for years, and never, never have they proved to be untrustworthy. No, no, I think we must look for the scoundrel outside of the house. Listen, I've got something to tell you: I spent the evening in the library on the first floor. I was sitting at the window, reading a good mystery, when I dozed off for a while. At about 10:00, a loud peal of thunder woke me. The bolt of lightning that followed it lit up the area behind the house. For a split second, I saw a figure with a small case under its arm, scurrying towards the fence. Then everything went dark again. You see what I mean, Inspector!"

"Yes, yes," I said and filled my pipe. The Lord continued persuasively: "Naturally, the fact that my butler was outside at the time of the crime does cast some suspicion upon him—but I can't believe it's possible. And the maid...no, no, she is much too nervous to have pulled off anything so daring...."

"Well!" I interrupted him—and I believe I must have laughed loudly, to cut the tension—"I think I've got it!"

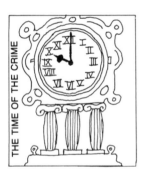 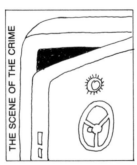 

Inspector "Comb" Brush paused in his story, and shot an annoyed, cross-eyed look at his pipe, which had gone out.

"Gentlemen, now it's your turn. I cannot claim that there is any one fact in my story that proves who stole the jewelry, yet there are some clues that aroused my suspicion. And as later became clear, my hunch paid off."

Brush got up and took his leave. He was absolutely gloating with delight.

A JUNIOR DETECTIVE WHO'S GOT IT

A JUNIOR DETECTIVE WHO'S HAD IT

SEE: SOLUTIONS ON P. 141.

Junior detectives who would like to either sharpen their wits further or increase their self-confidence may want to look up these whodunnit mystery books:

By Dennis Wheatley: *Who Killed Robert Prentice? Murder off Miami*
By Donald J. Sobol: *Encyclopedia Brown Shows the Way, Encyclopedia Brown Tracks Them Down, Encyclopedia Brown Saves the Day, Encyclopedia Brown Takes the Case.*

WITNESSES

A witness is a person who saw something that happened, or who can give a firsthand account of an event. Witnesses are often called upon to testify in court about what they saw or what they know. If a witness is caught lying, he or she can be prosecuted. Although this sounds simple enough, figuring out whether someone is lying can be quite complicated.

Just as no two people are alike, no two witnesses will offer identical testimonies. A detective talking to several witnesses has to unravel the real facts from the conflicting statements. And there are different types of witnesses: silent and talkative ones, nearsighted and hard-of-hearing ones, those who want to protect suspects and those who want to see them behind bars, those who have been bribed and those who have been blackmailed, those who saw and heard nothing, and still others who are dead sure they saw every detail.

Here is how three witnesses describe a bank robber:

WOMAN FROM THE
2ND FLOOR

WORKER FROM THE
SEWER

CABDRIVER FROM CAR

On the other side of town, a swindler went door to door, claiming he was collecting for a good cause. Private Eye W. later took the statements of three witnesses, who described the swindler as follows:

SENIOR CITIZEN:
He was very tall. At least seven feet tall. And he had a strong build. His clothes were elegant—like a banker's. He had an enormous, beautiful beard. He was courteous and had a soft, pleasant voice.

WRITER:
He was medium-height and decidedly fat. His clothes were like the ones you see in a crazy fashion magazine. Beard? No, at most he had a 5:00 shadow. He spoke in broken English—full of mistakes—in a slick, suave voice.

DELIVERY DRIVER:
A slight little guy. He was dressed like an undertaker. Had a highfalutin way of speaking, like a professor, although I couldn't understand a word—he had such a soft, thin voice.

Are these witnesses describing the same person? Yes. Are the witnesses lying? No. Psychologically aware junior detectives will know why their statements differ. (See: Solutions on p. 141.)

AND AFTER ME, LIKE A PACK OF WILD HOUNDS:
CONTINUED ON PAGE 137
THE ACTORS, THE DIRECTOR, THE PROMPTER, THE PLAYWRIGHT, AND THREE EXTRAS...

X: THE GREAT UNKNOWN FACTOR

1. The following problem should be solved even by small-fry detectives who are quite weak in math:

    100 X = 100

2. But even higher-level detectives may have a hard time with this one:

$$\sum_{i=1}^{n} a_i \frac{\sqrt[3]{x^{-3}(100,635)^5} + \sqrt[4]{\frac{36^{-4}}{394,604 a^2}}}{\frac{c(24816-3a)}{\frac{\sin \alpha}{b}} \; ; \; \frac{\tan \beta}{c^{(b-a)}}} + \frac{\int_{c}^{c} x \sqrt[-4]{\frac{15(6-b^2)}{3465,973}}}{\frac{\cos xy}{\sqrt[10]{763 \cdot 356}}} = X$$

3. And the problem below is a tough one even for master-detectives:

    Murder victim + scene of crime + murder weapon + events leading up to crime + time of crime + motive + fingerprints + testimony of witnesses + results of autopsy + unreliable testimony of witnesses = X

    Whereby X—the great unknown factor—stands for the culprit.

Sometimes the equation works out and the detective gets an *A*. Other times, however, detectives can't find the solution. Their boss bawls them out, they have to do overtime, their lack of success is noted in their service record, and their pay raise is cancelled. In other words, they are in the same kind of trouble as the small-fry detective who is weak in math and wasn't able to solve Example 1 above.

Z

ZACK, INSPECTOR

Last and least, there is Inspector Zack. Inspector Frank Zack. He's not famous or important enough to warrant space under **famous detectives.** His claim to fame is limited to a small fan club of junior detectives.

He can be found in this book under the entries **logic, scene of the crime—time of the crime,** and **pursuit.**

Zack and the author of this book go back a long way, but they aren't terribly close. Why, then, for heaven's sake, has Zack been included? It's as simple as this: he got into the *Detective Dictionary* by bribing the author with a cheap bottle of whiskey (see: **bribery).**

If after learning this very confidential information you still want to write him, here's his address:

> Inspector F. Zack
> Graschuh 41
> A-8510 AUSTRIA

CONTINUED ON PAGE 144

YET THANKS TO MY FANCY FOOTWORK AND UNDERWORLD CONNECTIONS, I GOT AWAY.

SOLUTIONS

Here are all the answers to the mysteries, questions, and riddles that were asked in this book. As a sharp-witted junior detective, you will need these pages, at most, to confirm your keen perceptions—and to give yourself, as they say, a well-deserved pat on the back.

ALIBI

Right—everything stinks here, even the question!

AUTOPSY

Exactly—after 1 and 2 come 6, 3, 5, 4, 7, and 8.

CRIMINALS

Have you taken into consideration that appearances are often deceiving?
1. Johanna S., internationally wanted counterfeiter.
2. Ed K., movie actor, here in his last film, *Some Like It Dead*.
3. Nicholas B., illegal drug manufacturer.
4. John W., butcher.
5. Carl Z., shrewd tax dodger.
6. School Supervisor J. R., on his way home from a masquerade party (he has discovered that he has lost his housekey).

HANDWRITING

Stupendous! The second signature is genuine. The others are shaky, stiff, or irregular in stroke.

INTERROGATION

Tom claims to have not heard about the bank robbery, because, as he says, he doesn't read the papers.

Then how would he know that the stash only amounted to ''a few hundred lousy dollars''? ($250 is absolutely small potatoes for a bank robbery.)

And how did he know that the robbery took place at 9:35 A.M.? Three cheers for the nonviolent interrogation techniques of Inspector Sneek! Three cheers for you, too (that is, if you solved this case on your own)!

LOGIC

Too difficult? Here are some tips that should help you—before you memorize the solution and show off to your pals, that is:

Inspector Zack first takes Albert's testimony. He crosses off the squares where Albert could not have been. (Don't forget—no one lied!)

	Football	Movies	Harry's Hamburgers	Naschmarkt
Albert			////	////
Burt				
Charlie				
Danny				

With Burt, it's easier, since he says clearly where he had been. Zack, however, also fills in where Burt was not, and notes that the others could not have been at the football game. (See Danny's testimony!)

	Football	Movies	Harry's Hamburgers	Naschmarkt
Albert	////		////	////
Burt	✓		////	////
Charlie	////			
Danny	////			

Have you already said ''Eureka''? Then don't read on, but do the rest yourself!
Here are the final results:

	Football	Movies	Harry's Hamburgers	Naschmarkt
Albert	////	✓	////	////
Burt	✓	////	////	////
Charlie	////	////	✓	////
Danny	////	////	////	✓

Danny was at the Naschmarkt. Surprise, surprise!

MOTIVE

Queen Victoria of England
1819–1901

Jerry Lewis
American comedian
1926–

Karl Marx
German philosopher
1818–1883

Marilyn Monroe
American film star
1926–1962

Kaiser Franz Joseph I of Austria
1830–1916

Evita Perón
wife of the Argentinian president Juan Perón
1919–1952

SECRET CODE

Solved? Congratulations! Not solved? Well, it really was a tough one!

YOU DID INDEED CRACK A CODE,
LOGICAL THINKING WAS THE MODE.
IMPATIENCE PLAYS NO PART,
FOR PEOPLE WHO ARE SMART.

SLANG

Here is one of the many possible translations:
Picture 1: All right, you fool! Don't move!
Picture 2: Tell me! Who killed Charley?
Picture 3: You don't want to betray anyone? All right, you petty criminal! I am going to hit you in the face until your teeth fall out!

SPELLING

Of course, you knew even without using a dictionary: CARPET is the correct spelling.

WHODUNNIT?

Just as you did, Inspector Brush noticed that the broken pieces of window glass were lying "in the flower bed outside the window." Thus, the window could only have been smashed from the inside, which means that the crime was executed by someone who was in the house (or at least had access to it).

Brush also found Lord Benston's testimony particularly telling: "At about 10:00, a loud peal of thunder woke me. The bolt of lightning that followed it lit up...." Lightning and thunder occur simultaneously, yet we always see the lightning first and hear the thunder afterward. How can this strange exception at Lord Benston's mansion be explained? Brush had to presume—with all due respect to blue blood—that His Lordship was lying. Could it be that the Lord himself was the thief? Yes! And since the jewelry was insured, and the Lord himself stood to benefit financially, this suspicion became a conviction.

In the end, Lord Benston was not charged with theft, but with insurance fraud.

WITNESSES

Way to go! You figured it out again!

INDEX

Words in **bold type** are entries.

agents: federal, 33, 51
See also **FBI; secret agents**
Alcatraz, 6, 83
alibi, 6-7, 80
Archer, Lew, 83
arsenic, 8, 93
autopsy, 8-10, 88, 100, 128

bail, 82, 83
bank robbery, 13, 33, 48-49, 59-60, 62-64, 82-83
Barker, Ma. *See* **Ma Barker**
Barrow, Clyde. *See* **Bonnie & Clyde**
Batman, 40
bean soup, 10
Beretta, 11
blackmail, 11, 52-54
Blomquist, Kalle, 42
blood, 12, 88
Bogart, Humphrey, 13
Bond, James. *See* **James Bond**
Bonnie & Clyde, 13-14
bribery, 15, 110
Brown, Father, 17, 41

Caesar's key, 107-109
Capone, Al, 15-16
Chandler, Raymond, 16, 44
Charles, Nick and Nora, 52
Chateau D'If, 16-17
Chesterton, G. K., 17, 41
Chicago, 15, 33, 92

Christie, Agatha, 17, 41, 43
clothing, 18, 50-51
clues, 19-20, 46-47, 102, 126
codes. *See* **secret codes**
comic book heroes, 40, 44, 45
confession, 23, 61, 90
cops and robbers, 20-23
coroner, 8-10
counterfeiting, 24, 60, 65
crime doesn't pay, 25
criminals, 26, 84. *See also* **gangsters**

dactyloscopy. *See* **fingerprints**
Dannay, Frederic. *See* **Queen, Ellery**
descriptions, 27-29
detectives: amateur, 17, 32, 39, 42, 43, 93; private, 11, 31, 43, 44, 45, 52. *See also* **famous detectives; training programs for detectives**
Dillinger, John, 33, 48-49
disguises, 34, 102
do-it-yourself-mystery, 35-36
Doyle, Sir Arthur Conan, 37, 45
drugs, 60, 61, 84
Dupin, Auguste, 39, 43, 93, 105-106

Ecke, Wolfgang, 40
evidence, 19, 30, 38-39, 90, 99, 102, 121, 126

Falk, Lee, 44

famous detectives, 39-45
FBI, 31, 33, 46, 49, 51, 83, 102, 126
felony, 57
fingerprints, 19, 30, 46-47, 77, 78, 88, 101
Fleming, Ian, 68
footprints, 20, 72
France, 16, 125

gangsters, 15-16, 48-49; famous, 13-14, 15-16, 33, 51, 82-83
gear, 18, 50-51, 76-78
G-men, 46, 51
Gould, Chester, 40
graphology. *See* **handwriting**
guns, 11, 82, 84, 118, 127-128

Hammer, Frank, 14
Hammett, Dashiell, 13, 52
handguns. *See* guns
handwriting, 52-55
Harlem, 55
Herge, 45
hijacking, 70, 123
Himes, Chester, 55-56
Hitchcock, Alfred, 56, 67
Holmes, Sherlock, 37, 43, 45, 126
homicide, 56-57
Hoover, J. Edgar, 33, 46
hostages, 70

identification, 46-47
identikit picture, 57-58
informant. *See* **stool pigeon**
Interpol, 24, 59-60, 97
interrogation, 23, 61-64, 79

invisible ink, 65-66, 77

Jack the Ripper, 67
Jackson, 55-56
James Bond, 68
Johnson, Coffin Ed, 55
Jones, Grave Digger, 55

Kane, Bob, 40
Kelly, George "Machine Gun," 49, 51
kidnapping, 69-70, 83, 123
know-how, 70-76

laboratory, 12, 65, 76-78
Leblanc, Maurice, 79
Lee, Manfred B. *See* Queen, Ellery
lie detector, 61, 79-80
Lindbergh kidnapping, 69-70
Lindgren, Astrid, 42
logic, 39, 68, 80-82
London, 45, 67, 101, 127
Los Angeles, 16, 44
Lowndes, Marie Belloc, 67
Luger, 82
Lupin, Arsène, 79

Ma Barker, 82-83
MacDonald, Ross, 83
Mafia, 49, 60, 84
Maigret, Inspector, 41, 110
malice, 56-57
manslaughter, 56, 57
Marlowe, Philip, 16, 44, 83
Marple, Miss Jane, 17, 43
Mauser, 84
Millar, Kenneth. *See* MacDonald, Ross
mini-mystery, 85

money, 15, 24, 83
Moore, Ray, 44
motive, 85-87, 110
murder, 46, 56-57, 67, 70, 93
murder investigation, 87-90

Paris, 41, 59, 102, 126
Parker, Bonnie. *See* Bonnie & Clyde
Pfiff, Balduin, 40
Phantom, 44
pictograms, 91-92
Pinkerton, Allan, 92
Pinkerton detectives, 52, 92
Poe, Edgar Allan, 39, 93
Poirot, Hercule, 17, 41
poison, 8, 12, 76, 93-94
police dogs, 94-95
polygraph. *See* lie detector
premeditation, 57
prisons, 6, 16-17, 111
pursuit, 96-98

Queen, Ellery, 43, 98

ransom, 69, 70
robbery, 48-49, 55, 57. *See also* bank robbery

San Francisco, 6
Sayers, Dorothy, 42, 99
scene of the crime, 6, 19, 99-100, 110, 127, 128
Scotland Yard, 31, 67, 101-102, 126
search warrant, 102
secret agents, 43, 68, 69, 103-104

secret codes, 21-23, 105-109
seven golden questions, 77, 89, 110
Simenon, Georges, 42, 110
Sing Sing, 111
skeleton key, 111-112
skyjacking, 70
slang, 24, 51, 112-117
Smith-Wesson, 118
solutions, 138-141
Spade, Sam, 52
spelling, 89, 118-119
spies. *See* secret agents
stool pigeon, 119-120
Stout, Rex, 43

tailing, 71, 74, 120-122
terrorism, 70, 123
time of the crime, 88, 100-101, 110, 130, 132
Tintin, 45
toxicologists, 94
Tracy, Dick, 40
training programs for detectives, 124
Trbuchovitch, Milo, 42-43, 98

Vidocq, François E., 30, 125-126

Wallace, Edgar, 127
weapons experts, 88, 127-128
whodunnit?, 129-133
Wimsey, Lord Peter, 42, 99
witnesses, 110, 133-135
Wolfe, Nero, 43

X: the great unknown factor, 136

Zack, Inspector, 80-82, 100-101, 137

ACKNOWLEDGMENTS

My warmest thanks to all those who enabled this book to be realized, and in particular to:

Gina, Jacob, and Maria Ballinger, Byron Citron, Ron Cole, Meghan Connolly, Irmi Formayer, Eveline Gans, Criminal Inspector Johann Gans, Ulli and Sandra Gölles, Maxine Hesse, Dr. Heidi Holzer, Dr. Peter Holzer, Inge Pock, Volker Rutte, Cathy Kerkhoff-Saxon, and Wolfgang Zwangsleitner.

For the illustrations not drawn by the author himself, the tracks lead to:

Batman Comics. New York, 1967.
Chandler, Raymond. *Farewell My Lovely.* New York, 1968.
_____. *The Blue Dahlia.* New York, 1976.
Chesterton, G. K. *The Innocence of Father Brown.* Middlesex, 1969.
Ecke, Wolfgang. *Balduin Pfiff.* Bayreuth, 1976.
Falk, Lee. *The Phantom.* New York, 1965.
Geist, Hans. *Gwendolin Klick.* Kreuzlingen, Vienna, and Munich, 1984.
Gross, Hans-Geerds, Friedrich. *Handbuch der Kriminalistik, I & II.* Herrsching, 1977–78.
Hansen, Walter. *Der Detectiv von Paris: Das abenteuerliche Leben des François Vidocq.* Vienna-Heidelberg, 1980.
Herge. *Tim and Struppi.* Reinbek, 1972.
Lindbergh, Anne Morrow. *Hour of Gold, Hour of Lead.* New York, 1973.
Louderback, Lew. *The Bad Ones.* Greenwich, Conn., 1968.
McCarty, Clifford. *Bogey: The Films of Humphrey Bogart.* New York, 1965.
Queen, Ellery. *Ten Days' Wonder.* Middlesex, 1966.
Robinson, Jerry. *The Comics: An Illustrated History of Comic Strip Art.* New York, 1974.
Simenon, Georges. *Maigret-Geschichten.* Zurich, 1980.
Solomon, Barbara H. *Ain't We Got Fun?* New York, 1980.
Steinbrunner, Chris, and Otto Penzler. *Encyclopedia of Mystery and Detection.* New York, 1976.
Das Buch der Kopfe. Munich, 1981.

96-104

363.2
BAL

Ballinger, Erich.

Detective
dictionary.

37327000100035

$18.95

DATE			